RAILWAY BYLINES

SUMMER SPECIAL No.4

Now, a *Summer Special* wouldn't really be complete without a glimpse of a Cornish branch working, would it? This is 0-4-2T No.1408 leaving Lostwithiel with the Fowey branch push-pull on 11 June 1956. PHOTOGRAPH: MICHAEL MENSING

Editor
Martin Smith

All correspondence regarding editorial matters
should be addressed to:
RAILWAY BYLINES
P.O.BOX 1957, RADSTOCK, BATH BA3 5YJ
Tel: 01373-812048 (office hours only
please)
Fax: 01373-0813610
E-mail: smudger@ivycot49.freeserve.co.uk
Views expressed by contributors are not necessarily those of
the editor or publisher. Information is published in good
faith, but no liability can be accepted for loss or
inconvenience arising from error or omission.
The editor will be pleased to consider contributions
(articles, photographs or whatever) for publication but,
while every reasonable care will be taken, no responsibility
can be accepted for loss or damage, howsoever caused.
In the case of manuscripts submitted for publication,
the editor reserves the right to amend the text, if necessary,
to suit the style of the magazine. Where possible, edited/
amended texts will be returned to the contributor for his/her
approval, but the final decision rests with the editor.

**RAILWAY BYLINES is published monthly
by Irwell Press Ltd., 59a High Street,
Clophill, Beds MK45 4BE.
Printed by The Amadeus Press,
Cleckheaton, BD19 4TQ
All distribution enquiries regarding the
NEWSTRADE and MODEL SHOPS should
be directed to Owen Eyles, PO Box 464,
Berkhamsted, Herts HP4 2UR.
COPYRIGHT IRWELL PRESS 2001
ALL RIGHTS RESERVED**

CONTENTS

Main cover photo. An NCB engine on BR lines...
NCB No.10 passes Fawcett Street Junction
'box in Sunderland with a train for South Dock
on 20 August 1965. PHOTOGRAPH:
IAN S.CARR

Upper cover photo. Little engines R Us... E4
No.62789 approaches Trumpington signal box
with a Cambridge-Mark's Tey-Colchester
train on 1 December 1956. PHOTOGRAPH:
J.A.COILEY

Photo right. Lynton & Barnstaple No.760 EXE
at Barnstaple Town in the early 1930s.
PHOTOGRAPH: E.R.MORTEN

Photo opposite page (top). What is the term?
Posed by models? Seems like it! But if the GWR
hired this dashing young chap to pose for a
promotional photograph (at least, we assume
that is the scenario), one would have thought
that the halt itself would have been tidied up
a bit and that the poor man would have been
given a half-decent set of luggage. (P.S: If the
gentleman is still with us today and if that
was his *own* luggage, we prostrate ourselves
and grovel all sorts of apologies for casting
nasturtiums!)

Photo opposite page (below). Mountsorrel
Granite Quarry's veteran Hunslet 0-4-0ST
THE BARON at work on 26 August 1954.
PHOTOGRAPH: W.J.FORD

Rear cover photo. Disused level crossing
overlooked by ruined castle – this is Dryssllwyn
on the Llandilo-Carmarthen branch on 14
November 1971, a little after eight years after
closure (the branch line that is – the castle
fell into disuse a wee bit earlier).
PHOTOGRAPH: ANDREW MUCKLEY

Welcome to the RAILWAY BYLINES SUMMER SPECIAL No.4. Yes – it really is summer. You can tell by the thunderstorms, the gales, Test Match humiliation (but England's Test cricketers are also humiliated during the winter, aren't they?), and yet another total lack of British presence at a Wimbledon final. But it isn't all doom and gloom. Relief – especially from those sporting blues – is only just around the corner. Yes… the football season starts on 11 August (at least, it does for those of us who actively support one of our local clubs rather than inactively 'support' Man U from an armchair on Sunday afternoons). But if you can't struggle through until 11 August unaided, all is not lost – this SUMMER SPECIAL will, we hope, provide some measure of assistance through those traumatic weeks.

Many of you will already be regular readers of RAILWAY BYLINES magazine (and we thank you for all your encouragement and support over the years) so you will know what we are all about but, for the benefit of others who are stumbling across us for the first time (you can recognise these people by their look of deprivation), we should explain that this tome is a king-size helping – an industrial-size dollop, if you prefer – of the monthly magazine of the same name. Each month, RAILWAY BYLINES magazine serves up 56 pages of branch lines, industrial railways, light railways, little locomotives, narrow gauge, Irish railways and the like, all for a measly £3.50. The magazine is in the shops on the last Thursday of each month but, should you have any trouble finding a copy, please don't hesitate to write, phone, fax, e-mail or send pigeons (addresses opposite) and we will try to point you in the right direction. Don't forget the name – RAILWAY BYLINES. It's the one which reaches the parts that other railway magazines don't reach.

Now, if you have any comments about this SUMMER SPECIAL, we would like to hear them. We always welcome feedback from our readers – you don't even have to be nice to us to get us to listen! – and a goodly number of readers' letters are published in each issue of RAILWAY BYLINES magazine. In the meantime, we hope you enjoy what's on offer here.

THE CONISTON RAILWAY
by I.C.Coleford and Bryan L.Wilson

'Coniston clusters around the head of a lake, whose beauty may be enjoyed from the railway that skirts there. Even more lovely is the view from the side nearer Hawkshead – say, from Brantwood where Ruskin lived. Green lawns run gently to the water's edge from the jumble of the slate grey village; beyond which, and towering over it, is a rampart of rugged fells. There are woods here in plenty, yet the keynote is ruggedness. The Old Man of Coniston, Tilberthwaite and Yewdale fells are a challenge to anyone with a taste for rough walking; and above Goatswater, three miles from Coniston, you will find Dow Crag precipices where the expert rock-climbers go'. (LMR Holiday Guide, 1954)

The area up on the hills to the north-west of Coniston had been mined for copper since at least the 1500s but the development of the mining industry had been hampered by poor communications. Quite simply, there was little point in increasing production if the ore couldn't be satisfactorily transported to where it was required. However, the coming of the Furness Railway in the mid-1840s finally prompted hopes among the local copper producers that an effective new means of transport was at last going to materialise. It did – but in an indirect manner.

The Furness Railway was incorporated on 23 May 1844 and opened its first stretches of line – between Crooklands (east of Dalton) to Kirkby, with a line to Piel and a branch to Barrow – for mineral traffic on, or possibly a little before, 3 June 1846. In February 1848 the Kirkby line was extended to Broughton. This extension was principally for the ore traffic from Coniston, the idea being that the ore would be brought down from Coniston, initially by barge on Coniston Water (the barges used for this traffic were constructed by John Wilkinson of Ironbridge fame), then transhipped to road and carted down to Broughton. The Furness Railway clearly saw the potential of the ore traffic: on 12 December 1848 it agreed to carry Coniston ore for no more than 3/6d per ton and announced that it was going to spend the hefty sum of £500 on improving the road between Broughton and Coniston. These days, the prospect of a railway company shelling out for road improvements sounds quite bizarre but, in the 1840s, a good road (few roads could be termed 'good' in those days) could be a very useful feeder for a railway.

Although the extension to Broughton had been intended principally for ore traffic, public passenger services were also provided. The line was inspected by the Board of Trade (a legal requirement before fare-paying passengers could be carried) on 23 February 1848 and, as far as can be determined, the passenger services commenced on 1 March.

In 1849 there were proposals for a metre gauge railway between Broughton and Coniston, but this came to naught. Presumably the improved road was considered adequate to meet most requirements.

On the standard gauge front, in 1850 there was a new addition to the local railway map. On 1 November of that year the Whitehaven & Furness Railway opened its line from Bootle to Broughton. This line approached the hamlet of Foxfield (which at that time, did not have a station) from the west and curved to the north to join the existing Barrow-Broughton line about a ¼-mile or so to the north of Foxfield by means of a trailing junction *(see accompanying diagram)*. Thus Broughton was now served, not only by Furness trains from the south, but also by Whitehaven & Furness trains from the north.

Meanwhile, back in the Coniston area, by the mid-1850s around 300 tons of copper ore was being extracted in that area

Ivatt 2-6-2T No.41217 came to Barrow shed from Plodder Lane in September 1951 and became a regular performer on the Coniston branch until the cessation of passenger services in 1958. This fine view shows the engine and the single push-pull coach at Coniston on 27 December 1957. Anyone familiar with the area will know that the Lakeland drizzle is not confined to the winter months. Indeed, Seathwaite in Borrowdale, a mere nine crow-miles to the north-west of Coniston, is the wettest place in England with an average annual rainfall of 165 inches. But we digress... PHOTOGRAPH: P.B.BOOTH

by promoting a nominally independent company, the Coniston Railway. The Coniston company was, of course, closely allied to its parent, even sharing some of the same directors, but by wearing the mantle of an independent concern it had a much freer corporate hand when it came to raising capital. The Coniston Railway was formally incorporated by an Act of Parliament on 10 August 1857, its capital being set at £45,000. Once the Act had been passed the company made little effort to maintain the impression of 'independence', its shareholders' and directors' meetings becoming little more than appendages of the Furness Railway's meetings.

Nominally, though, the Coniston Railway Company's first chairman was the Earl of Burlington who later became the 7th Duke of Devonshire. Some of the company's early local meetings, incidentally, were held at the Waterbeach Inn at Coniston. Although the thinking behind the Coniston Railway had originally been concerned with the potential mineral traffic, throughout the promotion and conception of the railway it was intended that it should carry passengers as well. It was also intended that the railway should commence at an end-on junction with the Furness Railway 'about one or two hundred yards south of the site of the intended level crossing at Broughton'. In other words, it was, to all intents and purposes, a continuation of the existing Broughton line.

Shortly after its incorporation the Coniston company invited tenders for the construction of the railway. The engineer's estimate of construction costs was £23,370 and the tenders ranged from £19,779.0.2d to £41,180.14.6d. The contract was awarded to Messrs. Child & Pickles of Bradford whose tender – the second lowest – had been for £20,907.11.8d. The agreed completion date was March 1859. The contract for the supply of rails was awarded to Messrs. Thompson Foreward & Co at £6.2.6d per ton.

The construction work itself was reasonably straightforward, but there was one particular aspect that displeased the villagers of Broughton. This was the matter of two level crossings within 30 yards of each other. This matter was one of those very localised affairs which are now long, long forgotten – probably even by the locals – but, at the time, generated considerable paperwork which, fortunately, survives today and provides a fascinating glimpse of 'how things were done'. This is what it was all about...

At Broughton there were two public roads leading to Ulverston. Rather than cross both roads on the level – the crossings would have been within 30 yards of each other – the railway company obtained powers to divert the southern one. Nevertheless, some residents of Broughton felt that even one remaining crossing was one too many and that a bridge should be built instead, and they asked the Board of Trade to intervene. In April 1858 the BoT sent along one of their railway inspectors. (The ensuing report bears the name of Captain Galton and seems to be in his handwriting, but notes have been added by Colonel Yolland and it is Yolland's signature at the end of the report – the implication is that it was Captain Galton who initially investigated, but Colonel Yolland later took up the case.) The inspecting officer reported on 14 April that he had visited the site in the company of '...Mr. Noble Jackson, the Surveyor of Highways, the Incumbent of the Chapelry and several other residents of Broughton, together with the Engineer and Secretary of the Coniston Railway'.

The inspecting officer noted that: 'The southern road leading up to the Town of Broughton has an inclination of 1 in 14 on it, while

each month. This was not a massive amount by today's standards, but it was certainly a very respectable amount – and well worth contending for – in the 1850s. The Furness Railway responded to this

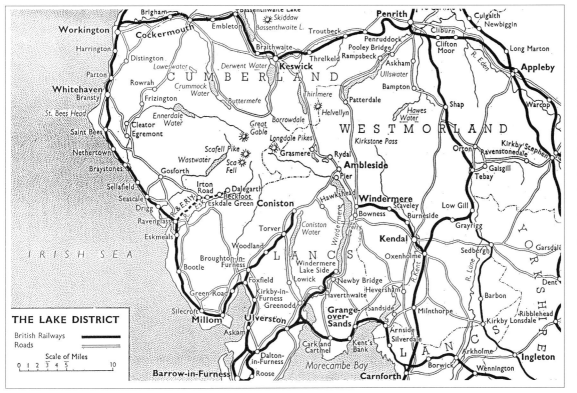

THE LAKE DISTRICT

British Railways
Roads

Scale of Miles
0 1 2 3 4 5   10

CONISTON.—Incorporated by 20 and 21 Vic., cap. 110 (10th August, 1867), for making a railway from Broughton (junction with the Furness line) to Coniston Lake. Length, 9 miles. Capital, 45,000*l*.; loans, 15,000*l*. Opened 18th June, 1859. This undertaking was amalgamated with the Furness, under an Act passed on the 7th July, 1862, 25 and 26 Vic., cap. 133, under the following arrangements:—"That the Coniston shareholders receive a dividend in accordance with the terms of the present working agreement between the two companies for the period for which that agreement has been entered into. The agreement bore date the 17th June, 1859, and was for a period of five years. The terms of it are, that the Coniston shareholders should receive no dividend for the first year; for the second and third years a dividend equal to one-third of the dividend paid upon the ordinary shares of the Furness; and for the fourth and fifth years, a dividend equal to half of the dividend on the Furness ordinary shares. After the expiration of the term of the working agreement, the Coniston shareholders are, under the arrangement for amalgamation, to receive for the then ensuing five years, a dividend equal to two-thirds of the dividend on the Furness ordinary shares; and after the expiration of that period of five years, they are to receive the same dividend as the ordinary shareholders of the Furness."

Extract from *Bradshaw's Shareholders' Guide* for 1869.

the Northern road which leads to the square of Broughton and thence on to Coniston has an inclination of 1 in 8. I am informed that the southern road has the largest amount of traffic on it, as might naturally be expected from the inclination being much less. These two roads at the present time unite in one a few yards East of the line of the Coniston Railway.

I was informed that when the Coniston Railway was projected three alternative lines were presented to the Lord of the Manor, who chose the one submitted to Parliament, and it is certain that another line might have been taken which would have done away with the necessity for the crossing of this road on the level. Even along the present line this might have been effected by carrying the railway at a lower level and under the road, but this would have been at a considerably increased cost to the railway company for the construction of an over-bridge and compensation to the owners of adjoining property, and an injury to the indifferent incline of 1 in 50 with which it

is even now proposed to start from the Furness line.

It was also said that Mr.Noble Jackson, after consulting with various residents in Broughton as to what he had better do, signed in the column headed "neuter" – as neither approving nor disapproving of this Railway – but it is certain that the Level Crossing is viewed in a very different light by the residents at the present time. (A memorial from the residents was later submitted to the Board of Trade).

The Incumbent, the Reverend Robinson, who lives quite close to the crossing, informed me that he entirely disapproved of a Bridge as it would have the effect of burying his house. And it is certain that an over-bridge could not now be constructed without involving the Railway Company in a very heavy expenditure. (The track bed had already been 'partly formed' and some rails were 'roughly laid down'.)

I was also told that a good deal of the traffic that passed over this road, coming as it did from Coniston, would cease when

the railway is made. I made special enquiries also as to the present amount of traffic and was informed that there was no further public conveyance on the road save a mail cart which did not carry passengers. The number of carts passing this crossing on the 1st, 2nd, 3rd and 5th instant was stated to be respectively 21, 19, 15 and 17.

Looking at the nature and probable amount of the future traffic on the Railway and on the road, and the amount of risk to the public crossing on the level (it was also noted that, at the last local census in 1837 Broughton had a population of only 'about 300'), I do not think that the Railway Company should be called on to construct a bridge. But I do think it very desirable that the Level Crossing should be constructed at the Southern instead of the Northern road as the approach to it is better and safer on each side...'

The brouhaha concerning the level crossing in 1858 was only one of the railway company's headaches that year. The biggest headache came in August when the contractors went bankrupt, leaving the works only partly finished. The railway company's answer was to take over the work itself, using local sub-contract labour. On 16 February 1859 the engineers were instructed to 'prepare drawings and obtain tenders for the construction of the station buildings at Coniston and Torver and for the gatekeepers lodge at the public surface crossings...'. Nine days later – on 25 February – the inevitable working agreement with the Furness Railway was signed.

By the spring of 1859 the Coniston Railway was almost ready for opening. The requisite Board of Trade inspection was conducted by Colonel Yolland on 25

The Coniston branch trains started at Foxfield. As we can see, the station comprised a single island platform but had a substantial roof over the down (Whitehaven) platform. Despite being something of a rural byway – hardly the most intensively used station in the land – Foxfield was kept in very smart condition, complete with flower beds and attractive gas lamps. This picture, which was taken on 10 May 1958, looks north. The Coniston branch push-pull train, with Ivatt No.41217 and LMS carriage M24460M, stands on the right. PHOTOGRAPH: F.W.SHUTTLEWORTH

As noted in the text, in 1905 the Furness Railway built two steam railmotors and one of these was usually employed on the Coniston branch. The engine units of the railmotors were the only 'locomotives' built at Barrow Works. This picture of one of the two railmotors – very probably No.1 – at Foxfield also shows one of the four-wheeled trailer cars (with a driving compartment housing a duplicate set of control gear). An ordinary carriage appears to be attached to the far end of the railmotor, but we suspect that this is either an optical illusion or that the carriage is merely standing there for the time being. As far as we are aware the Furness railmotors did not – and very probably were not man enough to – haul another full-size carriage in addition to the designated trailer.

May 1859. His report kicked off with the customary description of the line: '...8 miles and 60 chains (this was the distance from the end-on junction with the Furness Railway near Broughton), single throughout with sidings only at the stations and no arrangements whatever have been made for doubling the line. (It was fairly common for lines, although laid initially with only a single track, to be engineered to double-track width so that, if traffic demanded, doubling could be undertaken relatively easily at a future date.) Double 'T' rails weighing 60lbs to the yard in lengths of 18 ½ feet are used. The rails are fixed into the ordinary cast iron chairs, each weighing about 20lbs, by 6-inch compressed oak keys, and for about the length of a mile by iron keys and bolts... The ballast is said the be 2 feet deep, the lower half consisting of broken stone and the upper of sand and gravel... There are 21 bridges on the line – eight over and 13 under – all of which are of stone and brick or stone abutments with timber tops, with one exception: viz. an under bridge with stone abutments and cast iron girders 22 feet on the skew... The largest work on the line is a stone viaduct of 5 arches of 20 feet span...'

Colonel Yolland noted that: 'At Broughton Station a distant signal is required on the Furness Line; the distant signal now up on the Coniston Line, but not in working order, must be used as a repeating signal. And these signals should

be erected at a greater distance from the Station. (The resiting of the signals was intended to give train drivers adequate braking distance). The handles of the levers for working the through signals to be brought together on the Platform.

The station buildings have just been commenced at Woodlands Station and they are scarcely in hand at Torver and Coniston stations. The platforms and signal arrangements are incomplete at the three stations – Woodlands, Torver and Coniston. The signals (distant) must be placed at greater distances than now proposed at all stations.

The gates at the authorised Level Crossings and at some of the occupation crossings are not yet erected and lodges have not yet been built. Considerable portions of fencing, mostly dry stone walls, remain to be built.

The siding at Woodlands Station is incomplete... No turntable has been put up as yet at Coniston Station. In working the line it is proposed to use a second turntable on the Furness Railway at Foxfield Junction. The line is to be worked by the Furness Railway Company. There are several temporary sidings to be taken out and, if the ballast pit is required, it must be protected by signals in both directions... Some considerable lengths of line require packing and additional ballasting. The end of the line at Coniston is to be made secure by buffers or a bank of earth...'

Given the number of items which still had to be completed, it was unsurprising that Colonel Yolland declined to sanction the opening of the line. Nevertheless, according to the 25 May issue of the Kendal Mercury the Colonel had: '...expressed satisfaction' (!) and that '...the line will be opened as soon as possible'. Clearly, 'spin doctors' were around even then!

The fact that the opening of the railway was more or less imminent was confirmed by the Westmorland Gazette of 28 May 1859 which reported on the arrival of the first locomotive on the Coniston line: 'On Saturday evening last (21st), for the first time, the inhabitants of Coniston were gratified by the shrill whistle of a locomotive engine, which attracted a large number of people on Cat Bank to see it pass. As it remained for some time, they had a good opportunity to satisfy their curiosity'.

Meanwhile, the final touches were made to the railway and, when Colonel Yolland reinspected the works on 14 June, he found that most of his earlier requirements had been attended to: '...temporary fencing has been put up at certain places along the line where time has not admitted of he permanent fence of stone walls being completed and this fence will be kept up until the other is finished'. He also noted that: 'Wooden boxes have been put up at the stations and the authorised Level Crossings to serve until the station

The Westmorland Gazette of 2 July 1859 included an article entitled *The Opening of the Broughton and Coniston Railway*

This line was opened for public traffic on Saturday, and the day being remarkably fine, a large number of visitors took the opportunity of visiting that romantic and beautiful spot in our lake district. The event was not celebrated by the directors in the mode usually adopted by large companies, but the secretary – James Ramsden, Esq. – and Mrs. Ramsden entertained a party of friends at the Waterhead Hotel. The inhabitants of Coniston, however, were determined not to allow the event to pass off without some little demonstration of feeling, and decorated the Coniston station gaily and tastefully with flags and evergreens, and the village itself wore a lively and joyous appearance. To such as have not visited Coniston the following sketch of its attractions may not be unacceptable; and, probably, induce the tourist to take advantage of the facility to "take a run" there. Should the traveller enter the lake district by steamer, he will pass on his way the ancient ruins of Piel Castle, and Furness Abbey, the interesting ruins of which once magnificent are well worth visiting. From here the line skirts the side of the Duddon Sands, where many attractive scenes meet the eye, and where, should the tide be up, "gliding to silence with unfettered sweep", it will add much to the beauty of this portion of the route. The Duddon passed, Broughton is reached, where a passing sight may be obtained of Broughton Tower, situated on a slight eminence above the town, the residence of John Sawrey, Esq. The next object of interest seen is the vale of Coniston, with its placid lake, and, towering above, the "Old Man" – Coniston mountain – surrounded on every side by his rugged companions, amongst which stand prominently out the heights of Yewdale and Langdale Pikes. The whole of the scenery around is highly interesting. The village itself is situated about a mile from the head of the lake, and possesses two or three comfortable inns; and at the head of the lake is the Waterhead Hotel.

buildings and lodges are built. The platforms are finished…'.

Subject to receiving written confirmation that the line was to be worked on the 'one engine in steam' principle and that working was to be exclusively by tank engines ('until the turntable is put up at Coniston, which is expected to be done in less than three months time'), Colonel Yolland agreed that the line could be opened to public passenger traffic.

And so it was that the Coniston Railway opened to public passenger traffic on Saturday 18 June 1859.

The route

Looking at the Coniston branch as a whole, it effectively started at **Foxfield** station which was not opened until 1 August 1858. That date coincided with the opening of a new curve just to the north of the station – this curve, which formed a triangular junction *(see accompanying*

plan), enabled through running between Barrow and Whitehaven. The 'top' side of the triangle (part of the Whitehaven & Furness's original line to Broughton) was later taken out of use.

Foxfield station was at a bleak spot known as Foxfield Marsh, the hamlet of Foxfield itself comprising little more than a few houses, a couple of farms and an inn. The station had only an island platform; the original platform was just 13ft 6in wide but in 1879 a new 29ft-wide platform was provided. The improvements of 1879 included a new overall roof for the northbound main line, but the southbound side – which was also used by the branch trains – had only a canopy. The station house was on the adjacent public road.

There was a small single-road engine shed in the fork of the main line and the

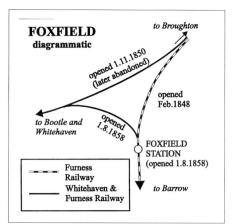

FOXFIELD
diagrammatic

to Broughton

opened 1.11.1850
(later abandoned)

opened Feb.1848

opened 1.8.1858

to Bootle and Whitehaven

FOXFIELD STATION
(opened 1.8.1858)

to Barrow

Furness Railway
Whitehaven & Furness Railway

Looking out from the station at Coniston, a Furness railmotor and trailer standing at the north end of the platform. Under the canopy is a notice advising passengers of the availability of Cold Luncheons, Hot Luncheons, Plain Teas, Meat Teas and Light Refreshments.

in 1897, a new up loop, platform and signal box were provided.

The line continued in a north-easterly direction from Woodland. It was still uphill, but the summit, 345ft above sea level, was reached near Dalton Road; from here the line dipped a little, but rose again to reach **Torver** (7 miles 44 chains). There was only one platform at Torver; there was originally a passing loop, but it was taken out of use in 1897. Also in 1897, Torver ceased to be a block post and a two-lever ground frame was installed to control the connection to the goods sidings.

From Torver the line descended for almost two miles – the steepest gradient was a ¼-mile section of 1 in 80 – but then rose slightly before levelling out on the approach to **Coniston** (9 miles 72 chains from Foxfield). Details of the first station here are not documented, but very shortly after the Coniston Railway was formally taken over by the Furness Railway in 1862, the Furness's consulting architect, Edward Paley, presented plans for a new station which was later described as having 'Swiss Cottage architecture and a magnificent mountain backdrop'. The station was further remodelled in 1897, the platform on the east side being converted into an island – thus the station now had three platform faces – and a new run-round loop installed. A new signal box was provided in conjunction with the resignalling work. Further improvements were made later; for example, the *Barrow News* of 8 July 1905 reported that the 'newly erected refreshment room is now open' (it had apparently opened during Whit Week) and that it offered 'meals at 1/6d' and was managed by Spiers & Pond.

Until March 1914 the station was shown in the public timetables as 'Coniston Lake'. This emphasised the railway company's determination to promote tourist and excursion traffic.

At the south end of the station yard was a single-road engine shed and turntable. It appears that the shed opened with the line but, as we have seen, the turntable arrived a little later. The first 'table, incidentally was a 42ft example. Initially, access to the shed was possible only via the turntable but, as part of the improvements to the station in 1897, the shed road was extended to join the new run-round loop thereby providing access from either end. The shed, as built, was a handsome structure with arched entrances and a slate roof, but in the 1930s the LMS rebuilt it with square entrances and a 'low-profile' roof with a full-length smoke vent. Throughout its LMS and BR life the shed was a subsidiary of Barrow.

In 1905 Coniston station had a staff of sixteen: station master, 2 porters, 1 signalman, 1 porter/signalman, 2 drivers, 2 firemen, 1 cleaner/fire-raiser and 6 platelayers.

Although Coniston station was the end of the line for passengers, in 1860 a ¼-mile long 'goods only' extension was opened to Copper Mines Wharf. This was a depot where ore, which had been brought in by cart, could be loaded by chutes into railway wagons.

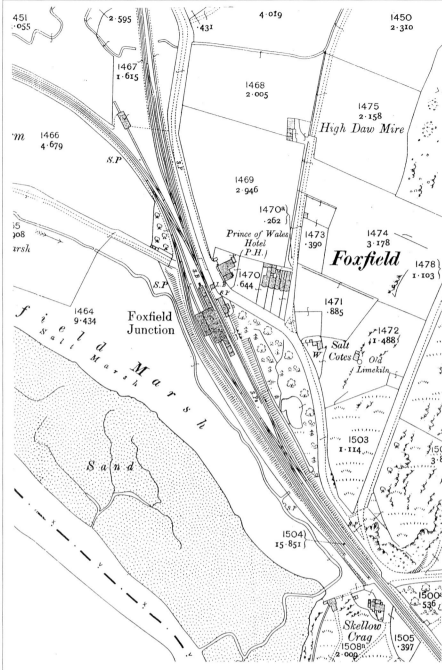

Reduction of the 25-inch Ordnance Survey map of Foxfield, 1913. The double-track main line to Whitehaven bears west at the down end of the station; the Coniston branch heads to the north. The building on the siding in the fork of the lines is the old Foxfield engine shed which, despite being officially closed before World War One, seems to have been occasionally used for stabling engines until at least the mid-1920s. CROWN COPYRIGHT

branch. It seems that the shed was initially the property of the Whitehaven & Furness Junction Railway (the proprietors of the Whitehaven line), but became Furness property in 1866 following the amalgamation of the Furness and the W&FJ. It is known that there was a turntable on the shed road until at least the 1870s, but it had gone by 1913. The fate of the shed itself is a little unclear. It does not appear in LMS records, but it is known that Coniston branch engines were stabled there until at least the mid-1920s.

From the junction at the north end of Foxfield station, the Coniston branch veered away in a generally north-easterly direction. It was on an unbroken climb all the way to the first station at **Broughton** (1 mile 22 chains from Foxfield) which, as we have seen, was the original terminus of the branch. For the extension of the

branch to Coniston the original passenger platform was replaced by a new platform. In 1903 a second, staggered, platform was provided to serve the loop. Another grey area concerns an engine shed. It has been suggested that, prior to the opening of the extension to Coniston, there was a shed at Broughton, but as there was a shed only 1¼ miles away at Foxfield, one suspects that the provision of another shed at Broughton would have been considered an unnecessary extravagance.

From Broughton the line continued its unbroken climb – peaking at 1 in 49 – to **Woodland** (3 miles 73 chains from Foxfield). The station was appropriately named as there was very little habitation in the vicinity. Woodland was initially a passing place but the passing facilities were taken out of use in 1884. However, when the branch was improved for the adoption of electric train tablet working

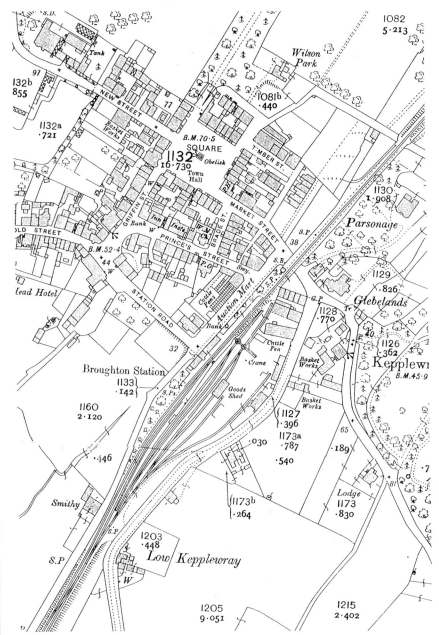

Reduction of the 25-inch Ordnance Survey map of Broughton, 1913. This map is a little misleading as it seems to show the railway being carried over the road on a bridge at the north end of the station, but this is, in fact, a level crossing. This is the very crossing which so vexed some of the residents of Broughton in the 1850s (*see text*).
CROWN COPYRIGHT

Signalling

The Coniston Railway itself was originally worked on the 'one engine in steam' principle with three block sections: Broughton-Woodland, Woodland-Torver and Torver-Coniston. The Furness's Foxfield-Broughton section was a separate block section. The signals at the block stations would have been two-arm semaphores, one for each direction, worked by levers at the foot of the post. The arms had three positions: horizontal for stop, 45° drop for caution and vertical for all clear. The lights were red, green and white respectively. The distant signals were rotating discs worked by wires. The manner of working was originally 'as per timetable' (i.e. if the trains adhered to schedules there was no need for any communication between block posts), and could be over-ruled only by a station master's written authority.

However, things did not always go according to plan, as evidenced by an accident at Broughton in 1861. On the fateful day, Furness 2-2-2WT No.12 (which eventually finished up on the Weston, Clevedon & Portishead Railway – but that's another story!) was hauling a passenger train from Foxfield to Coniston and, as was the custom, a goods van for Broughton was positioned in front of the engine – i.e. being propelled. This questionable practice had been adopted on the line in order to avoid reversing and shunting at Broughton as the junction for the station goods yard faced Foxfield. Meanwhile, Whitehaven & Furness 2-2-2WT OBERON had left Broughton station light engine. Her driver and fireman saw the Furness engine approaching but realised that, as there was the goods van in front of the engine, the Furness crew would not be able to see them. OBERON was immediately thrown into reverse, but this was not sufficient to prevent a collision. The fireman of the Furness train was riding on the front buffer beam ready to detach the van at the goods yard points – and this was where the collision occurred. The fireman was

This view of the north end of Foxfield station shows the imposing signal box which had been built by the Furness Railway in 1879. An entry in the company's engineer's book for January of that year refers to £500 for Foxfield Junction signalling 'in progress'. Note also the sturdy goods shed, the roof (but for one platform only) and the water tank. The station waiting room is in the annexe at the far end of the signal box.

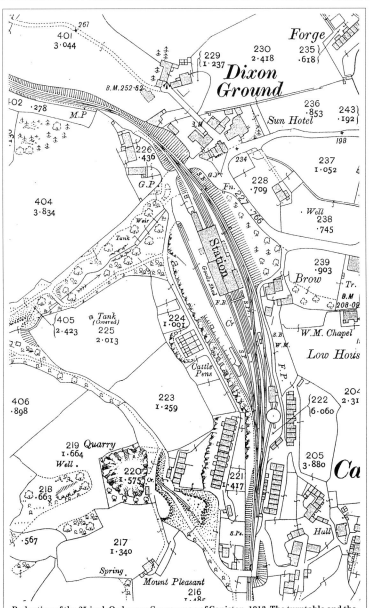

Reduction of the 25-inch Ordnance Survey map of Coniston, 1913. The turntable and the nearby engine shed can be clearly seen at the south end of the station. The continuation of the railway to the north-west of the station led to Coniston Copper Mines Wharf; this section of line was 'goods only'. CROWN COPYRIGHT

crushed between the van and his engine. OBERON's crew had jumped clear just before impact and were unhurt, but the impact brought OBERON to a standstill, after which the engine responded to reverse gear and tootled off up the line, minus crew, towards Coniston. Fortunately the gate keeper at Broughton was aware of the commotion and managed to open the gates to let OBERON through. She finally came to rest, short of steam, on the 1 in 49 near Torver.

Following the accident, the electric telegraph was installed on the branch in 1863. This was initially the 'double needle' system, but in February 1871 it was replaced by single needle instruments which used the Morse Code. During the 1870s the now-outmoded three-position signals were replaced by conventional signals worked by locking frames.

On 31 May 1897 the branch converted to electric train tablet operation, using Tyers No.6 instruments. Tablet working continued until 1958 when the branch passenger services were withdrawn. The line remained open to goods traffic until 1962, being worked once again on the 'one engine in steam' principle.

Services

After the opening of the Coniston line on 18 June 1859, the first timetable advertised four return trips between Foxfield and Coniston each weekday with an additional Foxfield-Broughton train in the morning and a return in the evening. On 22 June 1859 – the Tuesday after opening day – an excursion train brought members of the Ulverston National and Town Bank Sunday Schools to Coniston. Also present were 30 children from Ulverston Workhouse; they were treated to the day out by H.W.Askew of Conishead Priory. The whole ensemble amounted to around 1,000 persons. The excursion train set out from Ulverston at 11.30am and arrived at Coniston soon after

Looking out from the north end of Foxfield station, the main line to Whitehaven curves away to the left. The divergence of the Coniston branch to the right is obscured by the signal box. The building straight ahead in the distance is the old engine shed. It seems to have been officially closed before 1923, though it is known to have been very occasionally used for stabling purposes for some time after. Nevertheless, the building survived very well indeed – this picture was taken on 10 May 1958. Another point to note is the somewhat flaccid ex-Furness signal. PHOTOGRAPH: F.W.SHUTTLEWORTH

Broughton-in-Furness station on 17 June 1962 – this was six weeks after the complete closure of the line. There are some fine buildings, with the signal box and level crossing at the north end. The boarded crossing led to the staggered up platform which was completed on 8 July 1903 to serve the loop line. Despite this facility, up trains invariably used the main platform. The station buildings are now a private dwelling. PHOTOGRAPH: RON HERBERT

1.00pm. It returned at 7.00pm. The *Kendal Mercury* reported that 'The passengers filled every (spare) carriage at the disposal of the Furness Railway' – some thirty vehicles in all.

Later in 1859 the Furness Railway inaugurated a steamer service on Coniston Water. At that time the company did not have the necessary powers to operate such a service so the vessel was registered in the name of James Ramsden, their chairman. The vessel was named GONDOLA and could accommodate 225 passengers; she continued to provide pleasure trips on Coniston Water and was later sold to become a houseboat.

The inevitable formal amalgamation between the Coniston Railway and the Furness Railway finally took place on 7 July 1862. By 1867 the basic passenger service on the Coniston line comprised five trains each way, some of which called at Woodland and Torver only as required. By this time there had been a role reversal

What a specimen! The 14-lever Broughton box – stone built with some finials and an ornate chimney pot – was photographed on 17 June 1962. Immediately beyond the 'box is one of the contentious level crossings. It had once been suggested that this crossing should be replaced by a bridge, but that proposal was strongly opposed by Reverend Robinson who lived a little too close for comfort – he objected that a bridge would '...have the effect of burying his house'. PHOTOGRAPH: RON HERBERT

Woodland station, looking towards Coniston, 17 June 1962. In grander times it was a railway station and Post Office combined. The loop was added in 1897. Behind the 17-lever signal box is a siding. In common with Broughton, the station buildings at Woodland are now a private house. The station buildings are now a private dwelling. PHOTOGRAPH: RON HERBERT

between the main line and the branch – the Barrow-Whitehaven was now regarded as the main line and the Coniston line as the branch.

Although the Coniston Railway had been conceived largely with the potential ore traffic in mind, by the latter part of the 1860s the mines were in decline. Indeed, by 1874 – just fifteen years after the railway had opened – the ore was more or less worked out. This meant that the railway now had to rely mainly on passenger traffic but, in this respect, at Coniston the railway company had, to some extent, shot itself in the corporate foot. The two main copper mines at Coniston – the Bonsor Mine and the Paddy End Mine – were up on the hills about 1¼ miles to the north-west of the town and, in order to reach a mutually convenient transhipment depot (the ore being carted from the mines to the depot), the railway had been built on the higher ground to the west of the town. This meant that the station was a good quarter-mile from, and on the opposite side of the river to, the centre of Coniston. In other words, it was not altogether convenient for passengers.

Despite the decline of the ore traffic (copper mining ceased altogether in the 1890s, though from about 1910 there was some reworking of the tips and, later, there was some small-scale working at the old mines) the railway continued to handle a reasonable amount of general goods including flour, granite, coal, building materials and timber. In later years there was also some slate traffic. The Furness Railway also promoted tourist and excursion traffic, and although it was fairly successful – the company operated

steam boat services on Coniston Water (from 1872 these were operated with the proper legal authority!) – in the tourist stakes Coniston played second fiddle to Windermere. Nevertheless, various outings were regularly on offer. For example, the *Barrow Herald* advertised 'circular tours in Lakeland' via Furness Abbey, Coniston, by gondola on the lake, then via the Crake Valley to Greenodd. At Coniston, the coaches of excursion trains were often stabled on the mineral line to the north-west of the station.

When the Furness Railway's timetables were recast as a result of the opening of the Barrow Loop in June 1882, the Coniston branch boasted one non-stop train from Coniston (dep.1.30pm) to Foxfield (arr.1.53pm). By 1888 there was a through train to Furness Abbey (it was combined with a Barow-Carnforth train there); there was also a corresponding return working. These lasted until about 1892. By 1908 there was a through train from Coniston (dep.5.45pm) to Ramsden Dock at Barrow; this was, in effect, a boat train as it connected with a sailing from Barrow to Fleetwood.

As for goods services on the Coniston branch, in the early days certain trains ran 'mixed' – there were no separate goods workings. However, by the early 1880s the branch was served by a designated goods train; this was the 8.15am ('Target C8') from Carnforth and return. By the summer of 1908 the branch goods was provided by 'Barrow 13 Trip' which left Barrow at 12.05pm and returned at 4.45pm.

In later years the railway was also used for the 'export' of timber and slate. The

principal local slate quarries included:
• Hodge Close Quarries at Tilberthwaite, about three miles north of Coniston. As early as 1856 these quarries had been provided with a 3ft 3in gauge horse-worked tramway. The quarries were taken over by J.Stephenson & Co in 1880 but closed in 1921. They were acquired by the Westmorland Green Slate Co *circa* 1927 and the old tramway was replaced by a 2ft gauge locomotive-worked railway. The quarry remained in production until 1964.
• High Blue Quarry on the southern slopes of Coniston Fells. The quarry had a short internal railway – probably 2ft gauge – but an aerial ropeway was used to take the slate blocks down to the processing plant.
• Coniston Old Man Quarries – alternatively known as the Saddlestone group of quarries – on the north-east side of the Old Man. These remained operational until 1960.
• Tilberthwaite Quarry, about two miles to the north of Coniston. This had been worked for copper, but was later reopened for the extraction of slate.
• Langdale Quarry at Elterwater; although this was about five miles to the north of Coniston, some of its slate was carted to Coniston for despatch by rail. Interestingly, in 1896 a scheme was put forward for the Coniston & Elterwater Light Railway which was to run via Tilberthwaite and was intended to tap, not only the quarry traffic, but also traffic from the Elterwater Gunpowder Mill at Great Langdale. Unfortunately, this scheme did not come to fruition.

Returning briefly to the subject of the tourist traffic, in 1908 the Furness

Torver station, looking towards Foxfield, 23 April 1962. The goods shed and sidings were on the south side of the road bridge on the east side of the running line. At one time there was a loading wharf on the right-hand side. PHOTOGRAPH: F.W.SHUTTLEWORTH

Railway acquired a new steamer, LADY OF THE LAKE, to work in conjunction with GONDOLA, offering pleasure trips on Coniston Water. LADY OF THE LAKE was built by Messrs. Thorneycroft of Southampton and was transported in kit form, as it were, by rail to Coniston for assembly.

Furness motive power
As we have seen, the Coniston Railway had a working agreement with the Furness Railway but, in the early years, Whitehaven & Furness Junction Railway locomotives also appeared on the line, working in from the north. The majority of the early engines were 2-2-2 well tanks. One such, Furness No.12, which was involved in the accident of 1861, was a 'B1' class engine, but the slightly larger 'B3s' were also used on the line. Both of these types – and, indeed, virtually all the Furness engines delivered between 1860 and the end of the century – were built by Sharp Stewart. In the 1890s the well tanks were finally replaced by 2-4-2Ts. These new arrivals were, in fact, rebuilds of nineteen-year-old 2-4-0 tender engines.

From 1905 some of the services were worked by one of the Furness' steam railmotors. The engine units for these two vehicles were built at the Furness' workshops at Barrow – the only 'engines' to be constructed there. Each railmotor had seats for 12 First and 36 Third Class passengers, but two four-wheeled trailer cars were also built and these could each accommodate 28 Third Class passengers. The trailers had control gear at one end.

Furness railmotor No.2 had a rather brief life, being laid up after sustaining damage in a collision with buffer stops. No.1 did not last too long either. Although the railmotor concept was ingenious, the Furness vehicles, in common with most railmotors elsewhere, suffered from excessive vibration in the passenger section – this was an inherent problem of having the carriage section physically connected to the engine section. Consequently, the surviving railmotor (No.2) was withdrawn after only nine years' service, its boiler subsequently being fitted to the Furness breakdown crane.

Following the demise of the railmotors the 2-4-2Ts returned to the Coniston branch services for a short while, but were themselves displaced *circa* 1915 by new 'M1' class 4-4-2Ts which the Furness had acquired specifically for branch line duties. It is known that Nos.40 and 42 were at Coniston in 1920.

As for goods workings in Furness Railway days, the usual engines were the Furness's lightweight 0-6-0s, fifty-three of which had been built by Sharp Stewart between 1866 and 1884. These were, in effect, the Furness's standard goods engines and, on account of their origin, were invariably referred to as 'Sharpies'. These engines were distinctive in that they were paired with four-wheeled tenders.

The 1920s and after
By the summer of 1922 – the last summer of the Furness Railway's independent existence – the weekday passenger service on the Coniston branch comprised seven down trains and nine up. The discrepancy between up and down workings on weekdays was almost certainly accounted for by a couple of the down trains working in as goods only but departing as mixed. The first train of the day started at Coniston (7.15 depature), hence the requirement for the branch engine to remain at Coniston overnight.

Of the weekday trains, some ran through to/from Barrow or beyond:
• the 9.10am from Coniston ran through to Barrow and Ulverston
• the 7.45pm from Coniston (the last up train of the day) ran through to Barrow
• the late afternoon down train (dep. Foxfield 5.17pm) had worked through from Barrow.

Interestingly, the 1922 timetables also show an 8.25am Broughton-Foxfield local. At Foxfield it connected with a Carlisle-Whitehaven stopper; presumably the connection was intended for Broughton folk who needed to go to Millom – it was little use to anyone who needed to get farther along the coast in time for work as it did not reach Whitehaven until 10.00am.

In the summer of 1922 the Coniston branch boasted four passenger trains each way on Sundays. Of these, the mid-afternoon down train ran through from Ulverston (arr.Coniston 3.20pm) while the last up train (8.00pm ex-Coniston) ran through to Ulverston.

In Furness days – and seemingly for many years after – the mails were brought from Coniston early each evening to connect with the 5.30pm ex-Whitehaven at Foxfield. The 5.30pm ex-Whitehaven, in turn, connected with the 7.00pm mail ex-Whitehaven which had fewer stops and missed Foxfield completely. In the down direction the 4.40am mail from Carnforth *did* stop at Foxfield; the mails for Coniston could therefore be transferred directly to a branch train.

On 1 January 1923 the Furness Railway became part of the newly-created LMS. During the first ten years of the LMS's existence almost all the ex-Furness locomotives were withdrawn and replaced by LMS 'standard' or other absorbed types. On the Coniston branch the native locomotives (latterly the 4-4-2Ts, all six of which were withdrawn in 1930/31/32) were replaced by ex-Lancashire & Yorkshire Railway 2-4-2Ts. Significantly, these engines were fitted for push-pull working and, with the introduction of push-pull working on the Coniston branch, the level of services was increased to ten trains each way on weekdays. Four 'Lanky' 2-4-2Ts were allocated to Barrow shed, not only for the Coniston push-pulls, but also for the Ulverston-Windermere Lakeside branch. In 1935 the four at Barrow were Nos.10642, 10643, 10644 and 10646.

At this time the goods workings on the branch were sometimes handled by ex-Furness 0-6-2Ts, a handful of which survived into the latter part of the 1930s and two (LMS Nos.11628 and 11636) even lasted until the 1940s.

By the summer of 1939 the Coniston branch was served by no less than twelve passenger trains each way on weekdays. On Saturdays the 12.22pm from Foxfield to Coniston had originated at Carnforth while the 6.00pm return from Coniston ran through to Blackpool on Mondays-Fridays and to Morecambe on Saturdays.

As for the locomotives, by the latter part of 1939 only two of the Lanky 2-4-2Ts – Nos.10643 and 10646 – were left in the area. The reduction in numbers was because their other regular haunt – the Ulverston-Windermere branch – had had its year-round passenger services suspended in September 1939. (The services subsequently ran during the summer only, but that's another story...) The Lanky 2-4-2Ts were replaced at Barrow shed by ex-LNWR 1P 2-4-2Ts but, in August 1947, the same two Lanky engines – Nos.10643 and 10644 – returned to Barrow specifically for the Coniston services.

In the post-war period the year-round passenger services on the branch comprised ten push-pulls each way on weekdays and eleven on Saturdays. There was also an early morning Foxfield-Broughton and return. Interestingly, two of the up trains did not call at all stations – the 5.35pm ex-Coniston omitted Torver and Woodland while the 8.22pm ex-Coniston omitted Woodland. The first passenger working of the day was the 6.00am from Coniston and the last was the 8.52pm from Foxfield; the branch engine was therefore kept at Coniston overnight. At this time there were no Sunday services on the branch.

During the summer period there was also a through train from Blackpool Central (dep. 8.45am) on Tuesdays and Thursdays. The return working to Blackpool left Coniston at 5.47pm.

Another change of the 1940s – though one which slipped through unnoticed by most – was the withdrawal from service of GONDOLA, the ship which had been

built in 1859 for cruising on Coniston Water. GONDOLA was taken out of use in 1940, her business having been severely affected by the war period. She was subsequently sold and became a houseboat, but that wasn't the end of the story, as we shall see later...

BR days

Under BR auspices, it did not take too long before there was a change of motive power on the Coniston branch. In 1949 Fowler 2-6-4T No.42372 made a brief appearance on the branch, but this was not a long-term measure as, in September of that year, Ivatt 2-6-2T No.41221 was transferred to Barrow to replace Lanky 2-4-2T No.50644 (the former LMS No.10644) on the branch. During the week the Ivatt was outstationed at Coniston. The other Lanky 2-4-2T, No.50643 (ex-LMS No.10643), remained at Barrow to provide cover for the Ivatt, but in September 1951 a second Ivatt, No.41217, arrived at Barrow and so No.50643 was transferred away. Subsequently, the two Ivatts shared the Coniston branch duties.

As will be seen from the accompanying timetable, in the summer of 1950 the Coniston branch was served by nine push-pulls each way on weekdays; all of these weekday push-pulls were local to the branch – i.e. they did *not* run through to Barrow or elsewhere. There was also the early morning Foxfield-Broughton and return, but now there was also a late afternoon Foxfield-Woodland and return. There were also the Tuesdays and Thursdays Blackpool-Coniston services; in those days these were the only ordinary

Torver station, looking towards Coniston, 23 April 1962. The passenger facilities at Torver – a fairly lengthy platform for such a wayside location and substantial buildings – were on the north side of the road bridge on the west side of the running line. PHOTOGRAPH: F.W.SHUTTLEWORTH

CONISTON AND FOXFIELD.

This is the working timetable for the summer of 1950. Note that, apart from the 'Expresses' to and from Blackpool, the other services on weekdays were all motor trains. Another item of interest here is the 5.08pm Foxfield-Woodland and the 5.43pm return; by the mid-1950s this train ran only on Saturdays but now went right through to Coniston and return.

passenger workings to use the direct line between Dalton and Park South, avoiding Barrow. On Sundays there were three trains each way; two of these ran through to/from Barrow. It should be emphasised that the Sunday services operated only during the summer. For the rest of the year the Coniston branch was a 'Mondays to Saturdays Only' line. On the freight side there was still the thrice-weekly (Mondays, Wednesdays and Fridays) 'Barrow 13' trip which, by this time, ran only on Mondays, Wednesdays and Fridays. It was usually handled by an old Midland 2F 0-6-0.

Going back to 1954, in August of that year BR's lightweight three-car ACV diesel set was tried on the line. It was reported that 'running was good and schedules were improved on throughout'.

The railway company steamer services on Coniston Water were discontinued in the early 1950s, the last railway-owned vessel at Coniston being LADY OF THE LAKE. In marked contrast there were still five railway-owned vessels operating on Lake Windermere in the 1950s; this emphasised that, in the tourist league, Coniston played second fiddle to Windermere. Indeed, special excursions

to Coniston were by now very infrequent, and it seems that the very last was a day trip from Barrow on Whit Monday 1955.

The branch's uninspiring level of seasonal traffic was worrying, as the year-round local traffic was hardly plentiful either. There was, in fact, somewhat limited scope for local traffic as, even in the mid-1950s, the principal communities served by the railway – i.e. Coniston and Broughton – each had a population of less than 1,000. The next largest community, Torver, was credited with a population of just 196.

It was, therefore, not altogether surprising when BR looked closely at the branch's accounts. In 1958 BR claimed that the branch was running at a loss of £16,000 per annum (very roughly the equivalent of £½ million today) and its perceived solution was to withdraw the passenger services. It seems that little consideration was given to the possibility of retaining a summer-time service, as was still the case on the Ulverston-Lakeside branch. Although the branch hadn't been the most intensively used railway line in the land, the proposed closure was strongly opposed. Although the British Transport Commission came

up with proposed replacement bus services (provided by the Ribble Bus Company, of which the British Transport Commission held half the ordinary shares), the proposed route was along narrow winding roads – particularly between Broughton and Torver – which included climbs of 1 in 7 and, during the winter, were regularly blocked by snow. Such was the unsuitability of the roads that Lancashire County Council announced that they would apply for an Order banning the buses from them! However, a compromise was eventually reached whereby the replacement bus services were to be worked by suitably small vehicles and a number of passing places were to be constructed on the road. The TUCC, for its part, showed its customary amenability to the proposed withdrawal of the railway services, though it did succeed in having the closure postponed from Monday 15 September 1958 until Monday 6 October 1958.

A visitor to the branch a couple of months earlier – on Monday 4 August – reported that Ivatt No.41221 was working the branch motor trains with two ex-LMS non-corridors. The 2.05pm to Coniston 'carried about enough passengers to fill the average Ribble single-decker to the point of standing' and the 3.25pm from Coniston was almost as well filled. It was noted that very few passengers joined or alighted at the intermediate stations. Our visitor also reported that 'the shed at Coniston is a dry-walled structure, probably the only one of its type in use as the dry-walled shed at Windermere has been closed for many years'.

The cessation of passenger services was implemented as planned in October 1958, and in the absence of Sunday services at that time of year the last trains ran on Saturday 4th. It proved to be a case of bad timing. The service withdrawal more or less coincided with the opening of a new secondary school at Coniston and, as the school had a fairly wide catchment area, many of the pupils had to travel several miles; in the absence of any rail services the pupils had to travel by bus. This, of course, brought a significant amount of additional traffic to the inadequate roads.

As for the ordinary bus services which replaced the branch passenger trains, the Ribble Bus Company received £5,000 per annum from the London Midland Region

Table 165

CONISTON AND FOXFIELD

One item of interest in the public timetable for the summer of 1954 is the 5.08pm Foxfield-Woodland. It is advertised as a 'Monday-Saturday' service, but the corresponding up workings are the 5.45pm Woodland-Foxfield on Saturdays or the 5.33pm Coniston-Foxfield on Mondays-Fridays. It would seem that, on Mondays-Fridays, the down train, after arriving at Woodland at 5.17pm, continued as empty stock to Coniston to form the 5.33pm. We are unable to offer an explanation as to why the train ran empty from Woodland to Coniston on Mondays-Fridays, so we would be intrigued to hear any suggestions, please. But whatever the case, by 1956/57 the 5.08pm from Foxfield had been discontinued on Mondays to Fridays. However, it still ran on Saturdays, and now went through to Coniston (arr.5.31pm) from where it returned at 5.33pm.

The delightful little L&Y 2-4-2Ts were the mainstay of the Coniston branch motive power for several years. This unidentified example is seen propelling a three-coach push-pull set away from Coniston station; the turntable pit is clearly visible in the foreground. The date is stated to be May 1937, so the Union Jack on the engine's smokebox would be to celebrate the Coronation of King George VI on the 12th of that month. PHOTOGRAPH: ROGER CARPENTER COLLECTION

for operating the Foxfield-Coniston services. The LMR recouped only £2,000 in fares from these services so it still finished up subsidising the services. Given that the branch remained open for goods traffic, many questions were asked about the viability of introducing a diesel railbus service, if only at school times. But the questions were not answered. The cessation of passenger services was permanent.

Despite the loss of the passenger services, the Coniston branch remained open to goods, being served in time-honoured fashion by a trip working from Barrow on Mondays, Wednesdays and Fridays. The trip was now incorporated in Barrow 'Target 18' which served the St.Luke's Loop at Barrow, Dawson's timber yard (off the Hawcoat branch), Park and Askham brick works, before continuing to Coniston. The usual engine was a Barrow 'Jinty' 0-6-0 tank; Barrow had a fair representation of 'Jinties' at this time, seven having been transferred from Devons Road in London at the end of the previous year. The Ivatts which had

Ex-Furness 0-6-2Ts continued to appear on Coniston branch goods workings until the 1930s. This is No.11635 which had started life as Furness No.96 in 1907 and had been rebuilt in 1927 with an L&Y Belpaire boiler. She survived until August 1938. PHOTOGRAPH: F.DEAN

CONISTON

Approach.—By L.M.S. Railway *via* Foxfield Junction.
Banks.—*Liverpool and Martin's* (daily) ; *District* (Mondays, Wednesdays and Fridays).
Boats.—*1s. 6d.* per hour ; *2s. 6d.* 2 hours ; *4s.* half-day ; *6s.* day ; *15s.* week.
Bowls.—Yewdale Road.
Hotels.—*See* Introduction, p. 20.
Places of Worship.—*Parish Church, Roman Catholic Church, Baptist* and *Wesleyan Chapels.*
Railway Station, just above village.
Steamers.—Pier near Waterhead Hotel.
Tennis.—Yewdale Road.

The village lies near the western shore of Coniston Lake, at the northern end. It is a pleasant place for a summer sojourn, and a very fair centre for excursions. The steamers make frequent trips up and down the Lake. The **Ruskin Museum** is well worth visiting.

The **Church**, old, plain, and unpretentious, contains in its peaceful " God's acre " the **Grave of John Ruskin** (d. January 20, 1900). At the head of the grave stands a tall cross of the type lately revived from local models of the period before the Norman Conquest. The monument is of grey-green slate stone, quarried from the neighbouring vale of Tilberthwaite. The sculpture is illustrative of Ruskin's chief works. The church was consecrated in 1586, prior to which date the district was in the parish of Ulverston.

CONISTON (Lancs)

Miles 286¼.   Map Sq. 6.   Pop. 932.
From Euston via Foxfield.
1st cl.—Single 67/6, Return 135/-.
3rd cl.—Single 45/-, Return 90/-.

Eust. a.m.	Conis.	Conis. a.m.	Eust.
6 40*s*	4 24	7 22*r*	3 5
7 55*er*	4 24	9 20*f*	5 0
10 40*sr*	6 24	9 20*gr*	6 21
10 40*er*	6 33	11 55*r*	7 26
11 45*r*	7 39	p.m.	
p.m.		6 39*s*	3 25
1 35*sr*	9 16	6 39*e*	3 32
11 5*e*	7 3	—	—
Sunday Trains.			
p.m.			
10 50	7 3	—	—

e Not Saturday.
f Friday only.   *g* Not Friday.
r Refreshment Car.
s Saturday only.

ABC Railway Guide, March 1956.

worked the branch passenger ser-vices, incidentally, were both transferred to Longsight following the cessation of the Coniston pass-enger services. The engines' transfer has been recorded in the annals as taking place during the two-week period ending 20 September 1958. This was the planned transfer date (the withdrawal of Coniston branch passenger services having originally been set for 15 September) but, in practice, the engines were retained at Barrow until the revised date the following month.

In its 'goods only' guise the Coniston branch reverted to 'one engine in steam' working. The engine shed at Coniston had officially closed in January 1958 – i.e. nine months before the withdrawal of the passenger services – and this meant that the branch engine had to run light to and from Barrow each day. But despite its official closure, the shed continued to be occasionally used for stabling and servicing visiting engines. However, this all came to an end in April 1962 when the goods services were withdrawn, the total closure of the Coniston branch to all traffic being effected as from Monday 30 April.

In common with many other disused country stations, the three intermediate stations on the Coniston branch – Broughton, Woodland and Torver – were later acquired as private dwellings. Some of the old trackbed was used for road improvements, but much of it was converted into a footpath. Apart from the branch line itself, there is another well-known relic of the railway – or should we say the railway *company* – still in existence today. This is the GONDOLA, the old pleasure steamer which had been retired from cruising duties in 1940. She was acquired by the National Trust in 1966 and, following an appeal, was restored by Messrs. Vickers of Barrow. She re-entered service in July 1980 and has since operated on Coniston Water each summer.

Contributors' notes: During the preparation of this article reference was made to Coniston Railway and Furness Railway minute books, public and working timetables and Board of Trade reports; these were all sourced at the Public Record Office, Kew. Reference was also made to contemporary railway periodicals, especially the Railway Observer, *contemporary newspapers, and to signalling diagrams which had been prepared by the Signalling Record Society.*

Below. **The exterior of Coniston station, 27 December 1957. The building 'tacked on' to the far end of the station is the goods shed, while on the far right is the cattle dock. There is a pervading atmosphere of dampness; this is not exactly unknown in this part of the world, nor is the low cloud cloaking the higher altitudes. PHOTOGRAPH: ROGER CARPENTER COLLECTION**

With its two-coach push-pull set nestling under the roof, Ivatt No.41217 stands under the smart Furness footbridge at the south end of the platform at Coniston. Note the bridge number plate on the left-hand landing. The date is thought to be May 1958. In this instance the engine is hauling towards Foxfield; some of our other pictures show an engine leading towards Coniston, so there seems not to have been any strict rule about which way the branch the engine was to face. PHOTOGRAPH: PAUL STRONG

The driver surrenders the staff as No.41221 arrives at Coniston with the branch train from Foxfield on 5 April 1957. On the right is the cattle dock. PHOTOGRAPH: R.BUTTERFIELD; INITIAL PHOTOGRAPHICS

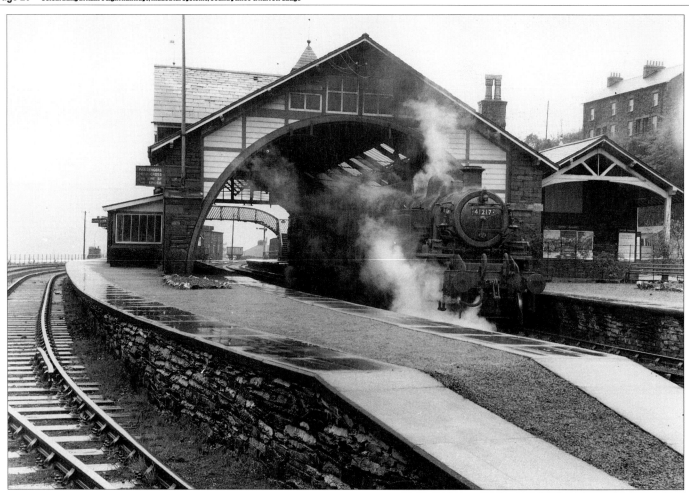

No.41217 simmers at Coniston on 10 May 1958. Its next job will be with the single-coach 3.25pm to Foxfield. Once again, we can clearly see why Coniston station was described as having 'Swiss Chalet' style of architecture. PHOTOGRAPH: F.W.SHUTTLEWORTH

The sturdy shed at Coniston, 17 June 1962. There can't be too many photographs which show turntable locking levers, but we see one here, complete with the maker's name on the quadrant. PHOTOGRAPH: RON HERBERT

The 'alpine' nature of the landscape beyond Coniston station is very evident. This picture was taken on 17 June 1962 – i.e. six weeks after the complete closure of the line – and although the signal arms have been removed, almost everything else is still in place. An entry in the Furness Railway's Engineer's book of 13 February 1896 reads: 'Erect masonry base for Coniston Station signalbox. To be of local slate. The upper portion of the signalbox will be brought from Carnforth where it now is, also the sandstone plinth course'. And here is the finished product – the 36-lever box of 1897. PHOTOGRAPH: RON HERBERT

Coniston North End ground frame of 1897. The Board of Trade inspection report refers to 15 levers, but only 12 working ones can be accounted for. It is an attractive building, completely at home in its 'alpine' surroundings. The line to the copper Mines Wharf continued to the left. PHOTOGRAPH: RON HERBERT

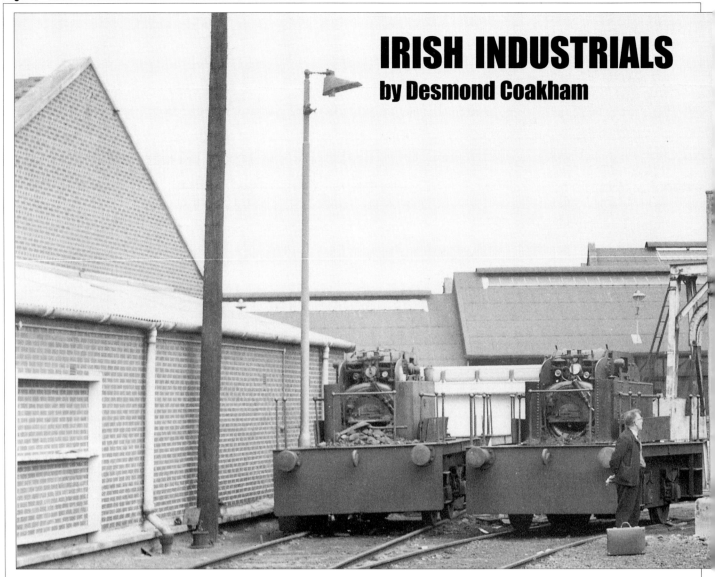

IRISH INDUSTRIALS
by Desmond Coakham

Above. Guinness's Brewery in Dublin was once almost as famous for its rail-mindedness as its stout. This view shows part of the brewery's own goods station; the two machines on the left are haulage wagons which enabled the 1ft 10in gauge steam locomotives to shunt the broad gauge yard when required, using a geared mechanism propelled by their driving wheels. *(See photo below.)* The little engines were hoisted on and off their host wagons by the shear-legs which is just visible behind the water tank. There was a marvellous narrow gauge network

right through the brewery, from a wharf on the Grand Canal on the south side (with a spiral tunnel on the way) to the Victoria Quay on the River Liffey. Here, barrels of the black nectar were loaded into immaculate steam barges, going down-river through the heart of the city to the cross-channel vessels at the North Wall. Diesel supplemented steam on both gauges before the system was abolished in favour of road transport in 1965. This picture was taken on 4 June 1964. PHOTOGRAPH: DESMOND COAKHAM

Bottom right. Guinness's two remaining broad gauge (5ft 3in) 0-4-0 saddle tanks came from Hudswell Clarke in 1914/15. Their journey from the brewery to Kingsbridge terminus (CIE) was through the streets (on wineglass-section grooved rail), so it was necessary for their wheels and motion to be enclosed, tramway style. Here, No.2 draws a train of CIE vans through Guinness's yard, past somebody's Rolls-Royce. Was the 'somebody' the VIP who ticked off the photographer for lighting a cigarette in the yard? The entire premises, inside and out, were a no-smoking area, apart from the Sample Room, where one was given the compulsory glass of Guinness. This picture was also taken on 4 June 1964. PHOTOGRAPH: DESMOND COAKHAM

Left. The photograph above shows a couple of the little 1ft 10in gauge locomotives mounted on haulage wagons. If you have a little difficulty visualising what these locomotives looked like on their own, this picture will clarify things. This is Guinness's No.13, built by William Spence of Cork Street Foundry in Dublin in 1895. Spence's built eighteen of these locomotives for Guinness's – that was Spence's entire output of steam locomotives. PHOTOGRAPH: PAUL CHANCELLOR COLLECTION

Heavy overhauls of the Guinness broad gauge shunters were carried out at Coras Iompair Eireann's Inchicore Works, where No.3 was photographed on 2 June 1951. She carries the green livery that was later replaced by the dark blue and gold colour scheme used on Guinness's road lorries. PHOTOGRAPH: DESMOND COAKHAM

The Londonderry Port and Harbour Commissioners operated a quayside-railway system that also linked the city's four separate railway termini, two of each gauge (5ft 3in and 3ft). The Commissioners did the obvious thing and laid mixed gauge (three-rail) tracks along the quays. Their steam locomotives were broad gauge with two sets of couplings at each end. It was not unknown for them to push and pull wagons of both gauges simultaneously, but in the last years traffic fell away and wagons were more likely to be nudged about by tractors. Fortunately, the two surviving steam engines were carefully put away. Seen here on 7 September 1963 before going to the Belfast Transport Museum is LPHC No.1, a typical Stephenson 0-6-0ST with 'ogee' tank, their Works No.2738 of 1891. Of the other LPHC engines, No.3, a product of the Avonside Engine Company of Bristol (W/ No.2021 of 1928), went to the Railway Preservation Society of Ireland. It was earning its keep in early 2001, ballasting on the NCC main line. Northern Ireland Railways had nothing suitable to spare! PHOTOGRAPH: DESMOND COAKHAM

Courtaulds, the pioneers of synthetic fabrics, gave the post-war Northern Ireland economy a boost by opening a large factory at Carrickfergus on the Ulster Transport Authority (LMS-NCC) Larne line. It had its own power station to which coal was rail-borne from Belfast Harbour, and its own reception sidings on the hillside above the works. Courtaulds used its own locomotives to ferry coal and empties between sidings and works. The first to arrive was Peckett 0-4-0ST PATRICIA (W/No.2088 of 1948). PHOTOGRAPH: DESMOND COAKHAM

The second Peckett to arrive at Courtaulds was WILFRID (W/No.2113), which was delivered in 1950. The two Pecketts were elusive creatures, the Courtaulds factory being largely out of sight from road and rail. It took a special visit on 17 April 1963 to obtain these pictures. When the UTA withdrew rail freight traffic in 1965, Courtaulds held on to their original agreement and obliged the Authority to recondition a large quantity of open wagons, mostly ex-NCC but some ex-GNR(I), for their coal traffic. This pleased enthusiasts mightily, but changing economics led to closure of the factory – and the rival one built by ICI – by the end of the decade. The locomotives were sold for scrap, and the adjacent Mount Halt, built by the NCC for Courtaulds' employees, was also closed. PHOTOGRAPH: DESMOND COAKHAM

FOURUM – GWR HALTS

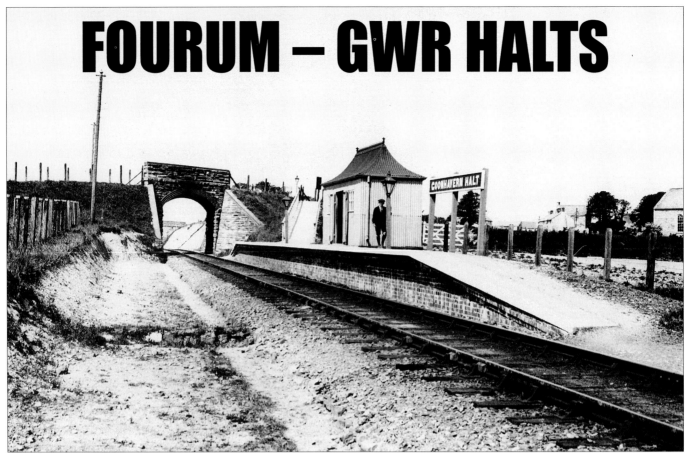

The GWR opened its first 'haltes' (as they were originally known) in October 1903 in connection with the new steam railmotor services in the Stroud Valley. The halts proved very useful as intermediate stopping places and attracted additional traffic to the line; furthermore, they were relatively inexpensive to construct (the Stroud Valley ones cost between £85 and £98) and incurred no staffing costs. Consequently, others were installed elsewhere on the GWR system. This is Goonhavern Halt on the Chacewater-Newquay line; it opened on 14 August 1905. This is perhaps the most familiar style of GWR halt – a simple platform with a distinctive 'pagoda' style shelter made of corrugated iron. This picture is dated 1922.

The GWR opened a total of 379 halts and 34 platforms (the latter being an even more basic variation on the theme) and inherited 40 others from companies it absorbed at the grouping. As we can see here, not all GWR halts were the same – this is Kingston Crossing Halt which was opened on 1 September 1906 between Chinnor and Aston Rowant on the Watlington branch. It has a small but smart timber shelter; the shelter was actually a later addition – this picture is dated 1919 and it looks fairly new. Also worthy of note is the low platform – because of the platform height (two other halts on the line had similarly low platforms) the branch passenger trains used to comprise auto trailers which had retractable steps.

Combe Halt was between Handborough and Charlbury on the Oxford-Worcester line. It opened 8 July 1935 – this picture was taken four months later, on 6 November. Little effort seems to have been made to conceal the origin of the materials used in the halt's construction.

After Nationalisation, British Railways opened ten new halts on former GWR lines. One of these was Black Dog Halt on the Calne branch, but this was not a straightforward case of a brand new halt being constructed. Black Dog had been built in 1874 as a private station for the Marquess of Lansdowne and until 1930 it even had its own station master. The siding there was used mainly to bring in coal and other supplies for the nearby Bowood House, the Marquess's home. The Marquess was amenable to the general public using the station, but the station did not appear in any public timetables until 15 September 1952. On being 'made public', a permanent member of staff – a Grade 1 Porter – was appointed at Black Dog, but remained only until 1960 when the halt became unstaffed.

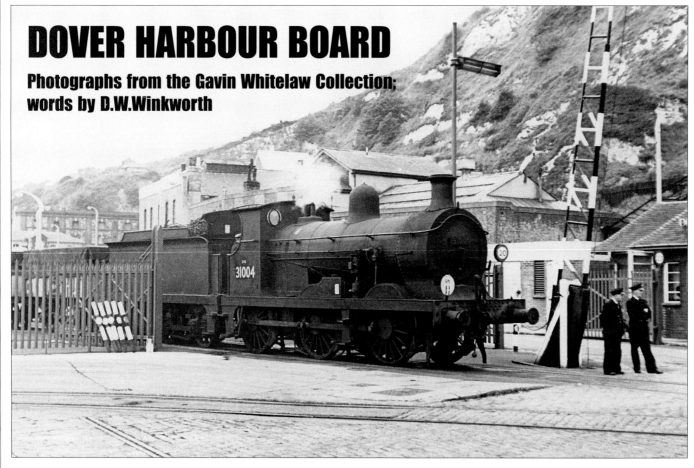

DOVER HARBOUR BOARD

Photographs from the Gavin Whitelaw Collection; words by D.W.Winkworth

From time to time an editor is faced with one of two similar problems: a text without any illustrations or illustrations lacking details or text. Where, as in this instance, there are photographs warranting reproduction the editor has to draw on the resources of his authors. In this piece, as D.W.WINKWORTH cares to call it (rather than notes or article), a sinuous thread has been found to link the pictures together. This explains the origins of what might otherwise be considered to be an idiosyncratic concoction.

The casual observer of railway lines in the harbour area of Dover could well be forgiven for thinking that the plethora of tracks were all owned and operated by the railway company. In fact the Dover Harbour Board (DHB) had an interest in various lines ranging from the Western Docks right around the Esplanade to the Eastern Arms of the harbour. Although the DHB did not operate any traffic over its lines, at one time there *was* some 'non-railway company' working at Dover – this was undertaken by the Admiralty who worked its own traffic over its own lines in the harbour area for a few years before withdrawing its engines in November 1923. The responsibility for maintenance of the Admiralty tracks subsequently fell upon the DHB.

The DHB's interests included the lines on the Admiralty Pier and the Pier Extension on the western side of the harbour. On the Pier there were two tracks for which the DHB received revenue and was responsible for maintenance, while on the Pier Extension there were two lines which the DHB received revenue from but were maintained by the railway company (later British Railways). Returning to the landward end of the pier, two tracks continued across the approaches to Dover Marine station – these were maintained by the railway company.Wany, no revenue accruing to the DHB.

There were various other DHB lines in the area of the Granville Basin and Wellington Basin as well as a major one, which ran all along the Esplanade to the Eastern Arm. An awkward feature of this route was the inability to run directly from Dover Marine or Town Goods to the Eastern Arm. All trains for the Eastern Arm had to be hauled on to the Prince of Wales Pier and reverse there, an engine being attached to the rear of train before it continued around a restrictive curve and then along the Esplanade to the Eastern Arm. Between the main line and the Prince of Wales Pier O class 0-6-0 tender engines (later O1 and C class) were used, but to travel over the restrictive 3-chain curve on to the Esplanade, P class 0-6-0 tank engines were employed, the larger engines being prohibited over this section.

On 26 February 1951 a new curve was brought into use, certain buildings having been demolished to permit this. The new curve obviated the necessity of taking the trains on to the Prince of Wales Pier –

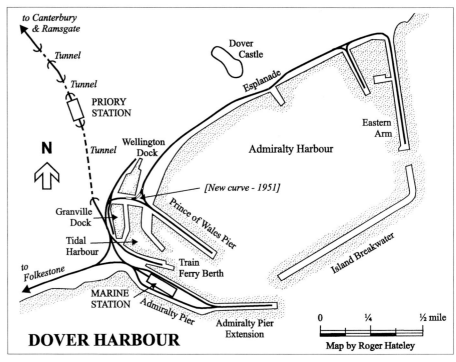

DOVER HARBOUR

Map by Roger Hateley

through running was now possible without reversal. Unfortunately, the new curve was of the same restrictive 3-chain radius as the old; had it been 4-chain radius it would have allowed larger engines to run right through, but the laying of a 4-chain curve would have required alterations to the Wellington swing bridge (across the entrance to Wellington Dock). So, despite the changes, the small P class 0-6-0 tanks still had to be employed. Trial running over the new curve was made on 23 May and 9 June 1951 and the P class tanks were duly passed for working over it. The older curve then fell out of use.

The new working arrangement was for the train to be hauled by the 0-6-0 engine from Dover Town Yard to Hawksfield's Sidings (on the west side of Wellington Dock) where it was replaced by the P class engine (and vice versa in the opposite direction). At this time about 22 wagons and fuel tanks were passing each day in each direction, but the little P class tanks could not manage such a loading and so an alternative form of motive power was sought. The outcome was that, on 14 October 1951, B4 class 0-4-0 tank engine No.30084 was tried alongside P class No.31178 on the Esplanade line. The B4 – one of the class which, in earlier days, had become so closely associated with Southampton Docks – was master of the job and was capable of taking heavier loads that the P. Accordingly, No.30084 was transferred from Plymouth Friary shed to Dover Marine motive power depot for the duty.

In the spring of 1954 it was decided that, to counter among other matters complaints of smoke and dirt from the steam engine, diesel traction should be tried along the sea front. However, it was not until 6 September that a test could be made owing to the repeated failures of the locomotive selected for the trial runs. This hardly seemed a good augury. The locomotive in question was DS1173, a 204 horsepower diesel-mechanical engine allocated to the chief civil engineer in the pre-assembly depot at Hither Green. It eventually carried out the tests of negotiating the 3-chain curve and hauling the maximum number of trucks allowed. There had been, incidentally, a suggestion in about 1951 that the DHB might itself obtain a diesel locomotive to operate traffic over its lines, but this had been rejected by the DHB as 'most uneconomic'.

The tests involving DS1173 seem to have been a little premature as, at that time, the Southern Region of British Railways did not have any engines of this type available. Nevertheless, a number were on order in the 1956 locomotive building programme; the type (later designated Class 04) finally appeared on the Southern Region in April 1957, but it was the summer of that year before Dover Marine shed was allocated a couple of the engines, Nos.11220 and 11223. The former took over Eastern Dock working on 23 September, being stabled under a street lamp in the Western Docks from Mondays to Fridays and returning to shed at midday on Saturday for the weekends.

Another of the class which was shedded at Dover was D2287.

The B4 tank, No.30084, was retained for two years until its withdrawal in August 1959. Eventually the diesel allocation was altered to Ashford where a pool was kept for working lines locally, and this probably gave a greater variety for the Dover locospotters. The class continued to work along the Esplanade to the Eastern Arm until 31 December 1964 when D2259 hauled the final train.

Top left. C class 0-6-0 No.31004 at the Western Docks at Dover – Wellington Dock is behind the photographer while Granville Dock is just out of view to the left. The Dover Harbour Authority offices are on the left. The C class engines and their ilk were not permitted over the sharp curves to the Promenade railway, so any trains destined for the Eastern Arm had to be handed over to smaller engines – P class 0-6-0Ts, B4 0-4-0Ts or, latterly, 204hp diesels. This and our other photographs came without any dates but, despite one apparent red herring, various factors indicate the summer of 1960 or 1961.

Below. In this view of Admiralty Pier the crane on the right serves No.4 berth, the Belgian vessel ROI LEOPOLD III is at No. 3 berth, while the containers in the bottom left of the frame mark the position of the end-on junction of the lines – behind the photograper the lines were maintained by BR, but between the photographer and the shore the lines were maintained by the Dover Harbour Board.

Top right. This slightly different viewpoint shows the containers to better advantage as well as grimy 2-6-4 tank No.80066 which is attached to an inspection saloon forming a route training special. In the distance, the pier running from left to right is the Prince of Wales Pier.

Bottom right. Dock shunter D2084 busies itself with boat train stock on the Admiralty Pier.

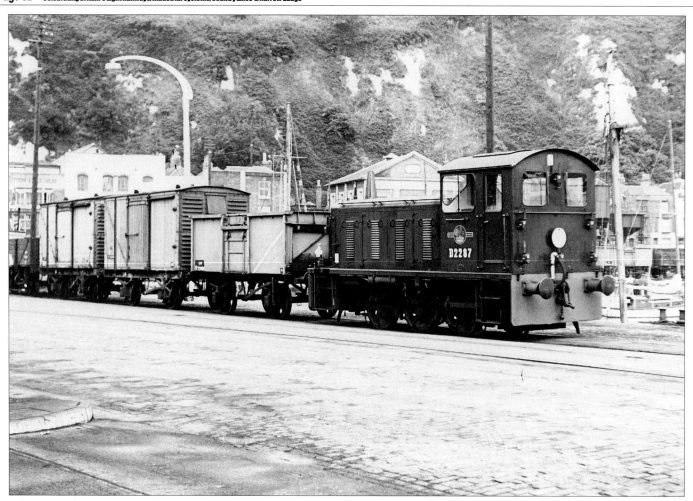

Diesel-mechanical shunter D2287 working in the Western Docks. Wellington Dock is on the right.

This is a much wider view of the scene in our opening picture. It shows D2287 at the head of a short goods train alongside the western end of Wellington Dock; it is possibly *en route* for the line along the Promenade. The buildings on top of the cliffs are Army barracks.

THE TALYLLYN RAILWAY – life before preservation

Photographs by Hugh Ballantyne

2001 is the Talyllyn Railway Preservation Society's fiftieth anniversary. In February 1951 they formally took over the 'old' Talyllyn Railway and on 14 May the first train operated by the society left Wharf station at Towyn. As a result of much hard work by the society and its members in the fifty years since then, the Talyllyn is now world-famous. And justifinaly so!

These two pictures were taken during the last summer prior to preservation, by which time the service was down to two trains each way on Mondays, Wednesdays and Fridays between June and October. The date is, in fact, 8 August 1950 and, although things had become, shall we say, a little rustic, the railway positively oozed charm and charisma. Our upper picture shows Towyn Pendre station; the engine shed (with DOLGOCH just about visible) and carriage shed are on the left. Our lower picture shows DOLGOCH – a Fletcher Jennings 0-4-0WT of 1865 – taking water from the pipe near Dolgoch station.

DIESEL DAWN – the LMS's Leyland railcars

During the early 1930s the LMS tried out various internal combustion railcars; among them were 'La Micheline' which had pneumatic types and the 'Ro-Railer' which could run on rails or on the road. *('La Micheline' and the 'Ro-Railer' have recently been featured in* Railway Bylines *magazine – Ed.)* Another foray into the world of railcars came in 1934 when the LMS took delivery of three vehicles from Leyland Motors. Numbered 29950/51/52, they were painted in unlined crimson lake with cream waistbands and skirts and the LMS crest on their centre doors. After various trials and public exhibitions, the three railcars entered traffic in July 1934.

The railcars' principal vital statistics were:

Engine: 95hp Leyland six-cylinder diesel engine with Lysholm-Smith hydraulic torque converter and drive.
Nominal maximum speed: 56mph
Fuel consumption: 13 mpg
Length overall: 41ft 1in
Wheelbase: 21ft 0in
Seating capacity: 40
Weight empty: 10tons 10cwt
Weight in working order: 13tons 2cwt

The three railcars were initially based at Lower Darwen shed and worked mainly between Spring Vale and Clitheroe. They seemed to be generally popular among passengers and railway crews alike. In 1937 one of the cars was transferred to Hamilton where its duties included trips to Lanark, Motherwell, Holytown and Lesmahagow. The other two railcars moved to Hamilton in the 1940s. The railcars were not at all popular with the shed staff at Hamilton; this was due partly to the staff's traditionalism – they were cautious of new-fangled machines which were foisted upon them by their 'foreign' management – and partly to the fact that, as the railcars became older, they became more prone to breakdowns. From the public's point of view the folk of Lancashire had had the better deal as, when the railcars had been fairly new, they had ridden well, but by the time the railcars went to Scotland they were showing signs of wear and tear and this manifested itself in very rough riding.

By mid-1949 only 29952 was in use – it was normally employed on the Hamilton-Holytown service. The other two railcars were laid up at Hamilton shed, some of their parts having been removed to help keep 29952 running. These other two were taken to St.Rollox in the early autumn of 1949; they were officially 'awaiting shops' but it seemed a foregone conclusion that would be withdrawn. No.29952 soldiered on at Hamilton a little longer, but it soon joined the other pair at St.Rollox. All three were formally withdrawn from service in April 1951.

Right. **The chassis for one of the railcars at the Leyland Works. The towing eye and hook in the 'buffer beam' is only a temporary fitment for moving the chassis around the workshops. Note the dual controls (plus handbrake) at each end.**

LMS diesel-hydraulic railbus No.29950 looks fairly new, but this clearly isn't an official 'soon-after-delivery' portrait as the vehicle has a dent on the corner. Furthermore, the roof is grey or weathered black – when new, the railcar's roof was painted cream. Note the lamp set into the roof and the lamp iron by the end windows. Note also the buffers and, between them, a small strut to which a hook could be attached; these fitments were not for the hauling of tail traffic nor for running in conjunction with other vehicles (the LMS's working instructions specifically forbade this), but merely to enable the railcar to be towed or propelled in cases of emergency. In common with some other early diesel and petrol railcars, their lightweight nature presented a problem in that they could not be relied upon to satisfactorily operate track circuits or treadles. Consequently, they were permitted to work only on lines for which they had been authorised.

No.29951 at St.Rollox Works on 31 May 1950. We believe that the technical term for this visage is 'seen better days'. As far as is known, 29950 and 29951 had last been used in early 1949. They had been taken to St.Rollox in the autumn of that year and languished there until being officially condemned in April 1951. A hook is attached to the vehicle's 'tow bar' – this would have been used for towing the car from one part of the works site to another.

THE SOUTHWOLD RAILWAY – an attempted reprieve
Notes by Seymour Blyth

The 3ft gauge Southwold Railway extended for 8¾ miles from Halesworth to the elegant coastal town of Southwold in Suffolk. It opened to traffic in September 1879 and, at various times during its life, Parliamentary Acts and Orders were obtained for the construction of an extension to Kessingland (powers for which eventually lapsed without any work having been done), the possible conversion of the whole line to the standard gauge (certain engineering works in connection with this were carried out), and the construction of a short branch to Southwold Harbour (this materialised in 1914). The Southwold Railway was not included in the Grouping and therefore carried on as a completely independent concern but, whereas the company had previously been in fairly good financial shape, this state of affairs was soon to change. In the mid-1920s, following the improvement in the local bus services the Southwold Railway lost a significant proportion of its passenger traffic to the roads. The company's fortunes took an abrupt nose dive, and this culminated in the closure of the line

in April 1929. Initially there was much local optimism that the line would soon reopen but, as the months, then the years, went by, the optimism dwindled. Nevertheless, the line itself was left *in situ* and the surviving locomotives and rolling stock remained at Halesworth. This situation prevailed until January 1941 when the Ministry of Supply announced their intention to dismantle the line and cut up the rolling stock to provide metal for the war effort. This was soon put in hand.

But that still wasn't the end of the matter. On 26 September 1941 – after much of the line had been lifted – the light railway engineer Ronald Shephard sent a lengthy memorandum to Baron Leathers of Purfleet, the Minister of War Transport, suggesting that it would be in the national interest if the Southwold Railway were to be reopened as a standard gauge line. Shephard reminded the Minister of Lt-Col.Moore-Brabazon's statement that, for the war effort, 'Everything on wheels is going to be wanted and going to be used'. He followed with a summary of the reasons (as he saw

them) why the Southwold Railway had failed in the 1920s:

• Over-capitalisation for the purposes of carrying out works and extensions which proved to be non-revenue earning.

• Maintaining a London office, with the Manager more frequently in London than on the spot.

• The Board of Directors did not include anybody with local interests.

• No Post Office telephone was installed in the offices at Southwold, and therefore there was no quick method of communication between the company in Southwold and the management in the London office.

• The timetable was not adjusted to suit local requirements and to connect with LNER trains.

• The extreme discomfort of the passenger rolling stock discouraged passengers from travelling, and when road competition presented a quicker and more comfortable means of transport it was not surprising that passengers availed themselves of it. The Southwold Railway's passenger coaches offered only uncomfortable wooden benches, with no

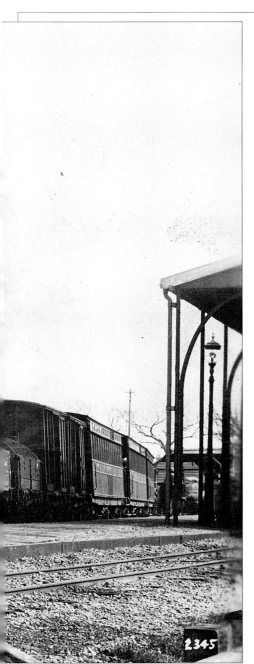

Left. 2-4-2T No.1 SOUTHWOLD was built by Sharp Stewart in 1893 as a belated replacement for the Southwold's original No.1 which had been returned to the makers during a period when the railway company had been a little tight for cash. This picture was taken at Southwold – note the single central buffer, the mixed train and the low platform. PHOTOGRAPH: ERIC ASHTON COLLECTION

Below. Back in the days when the Southwold Railway was a thriving (well, relatively speaking) 3ft gauge line, one of its 2-4-0Ts has just brought a mixed train into Halesworth. It is standing at the Southwold's island platform which was on the east side of the Great Eastern station. The GER goods yard can be seen in the distance on the right. The date is thought to be 1911. Although Ronald Shephard's lengthy memorandum of 1941 was about the reopening of the railway, if the scheme had come to fruition this sort of scene would *not* have been recreated as Shephard's proposals involved rebuilding the Southwold as a standard gauge line. PHOTOGRAPH: ERIC ASHTON COLLECTION

heating or lighting, and as no continuous brakes were fitted all trains were limited to 16mph.

• There were no facilities for transferring freight from standard to narrow gauge wagons at Halesworth, except by hand, a very slow and expensive process. Even coal had to be transhipped by shovel.

• The company apparently made no attempt to combat road competition by the use of lifting appliances, goods containers and employment of transporter wagons to enable standard gauge wagons to be transported to Southwold for unloading, or by attending to the comfort and convenience of passengers by adjusting fares and timetables to meet the bus competition.

In his memorandum, Shephard suggested that the rebuilding of the railway to the standard gauge would require '…only a small amount of permanent way' but he conceded that '…sleepers may present a problem but concrete ones are obtainable'. He also suggested that '…military troops might be employed in rebuilding the railway, thereby giving excellent opportunities for training'. Shephard produced letters of support from Southwold Town Council, the parish councils of Walberswick, Blythburgh, Wenhaston and Holton, and

Halesworth Urban District Council; he also produced a petition signed by 2,072 residents – this figure could have been higher but, Shephard explained, '…owing to enemy action the signatures of approximately 500 further residents have been destroyed'.

Shephard acknowledged that certain defence works had been erected on the railway, or so close as to foul the track, but noted that '…some of them appear to be disused and falling to pieces… and they will all have to be moved as soon as possible and any earthworks on or adjacent to the railway made good'. Furthermore, some railway property had been requisitioned by the military, the entire station buildings at Halesworth, Wenhaston, Blythburgh and Walberswick had been removed, some fixtures had gone from Southwold station, much of the permanent way had already been lifted (the job was completed the following January), two bridges had been dismantled and the rolling stock had been removed from Halesworth. Shephard's memorandum included his summary of the engineering work which would be required if the line were to reopen:

*'**Halesworth:** If it is required to use the overbridge at Halesworth it will have to be repaired and repainted. A new station shed*

A splendid portrait of 2-4-0T No.2 HALESWORTH outside the engine shed at Southwold. The engine had been built by Sharp Stewart in 1879 and was given major overhauls at Stratford in 1887 and 1895, at Southwold in 1901 (new boiler), at Stratford in 1910 and at Southwold in 1920 (another new boiler). It was cut up by the demolition contractors, Thos.W.Ward, in 1941, twelve years after it had last worked. PHOTOGRAPH: J.W.ARMSTRONG TRUST

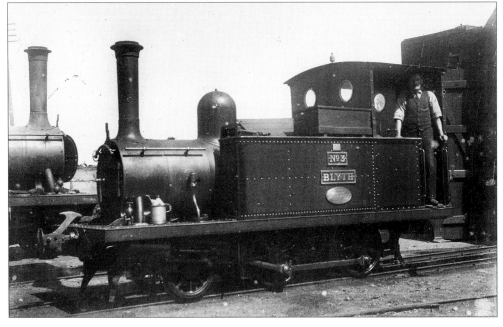

No.3 BLYTH at Southwold shed. This engine was also built in 1879 and was treated to four major overhauls at Stratford and two at Southwold. The two at Southwold – one in 1900 and the other in 1925 – both involved the fitting of a new boiler. In common with HALESWORTH, BLYTH was cut up by Ward's in 1941. PHOTOGRAPH: J.W.ARMSTRONG TRUST

and office will have to be provided. Damage to be made good and station premises and sidings to be cleaned up generally. Transfer shed to be made good or scrapped...

Wenhaston Mill: *The private siding here should be made good. Consideration to be given to realignment of the tack so as to reduce the number of bridges and ease the curvature of he line.*

Wenhaston station: *A small lock-up shed to be provided. The crossing gates to be either removed, repaired, or replaced by cattle guards. The sidings to be put in order. The entire station yard to be tidied up.*

Blythburgh station: *The station yard to be tidied up and the sidings to be put in order. A small lock-up shed to be provided.*

Walberswick station: *Site to be tidied up and the siding put in order, unless it is decided to move the station to the proposed new site at Eastwood Lodge Farm... The proposed new site is admirably suited for the purpose and would not interfere with the farm, the ground being heathland of little agricultural value. As an alternative the railway could be realigned from Eastwood Lodge Farm passing closer to Walberswick.*

Southwold: *The station buildings require minor repairs and repainting. The goods shed needs new timber staging and roof. The entire goods yard required tidying up. If the engine depot is transferred to Halesworth, the locomotive shed at Southwold can be demolished'.*

Shephard recommended that, if the Southwold Railway were to be revived, the board of directors should be drawn, as far as possible, from businessmen living in the neighbourhood and that the head office should be at Southwold, not London. It was also suggested that local deliveries at Southwold and Reydon should be made by a railway-owned horse and cart, while local collections and deliveries at Wenhaston, Blythburgh and Walberswick should be undertaken by existing local carriers who had already expressed a desire to co-operate. It was acknowledged that, since the closure of the Southwold Railway in 1929, the LNER had distributed goods to the local villages by lorry, but Shephard was confident that, if the railway were to reopen, the LNER would be willing to gradually withdraw its lorry service.

As for the prospects for the 'new' Southwold Railway, it was suggested that milk traffic would become a good source of revenue especially if the railway were extended directly into the United Dairies depot at Halesworth. Then there was coal traffic – it was estimated that the railway would capture at least 90% of the local coal traffic as '...the Southwold coal merchants at present have the highly unsatisfactory method of journeying about twelve miles or more to near Lowestoft for their supplies'. It was anticipated that coal traffic for Southwold gas works could also be secured and that, as the gas works was adjacent to the railway, it would not be too costly to lay a short siding directly into the works. The potential coal traffic was, in fact, considerable: during 1940 the Southwold Gas Company used 2,000 tons, local domestic use accounted for another 4,900 tons, and local industry used 378 tons.

Although Shephard's memorandum did not make any specific reference to locomotives, it was understood that, if the Southwold were to reopen as a standard gauge line, a lightweight locomotive such as a Sentinel would be hired from the LNER. The LNER had already supplied locomotives to other private railways such as the Easingwold and the Derwent Valley, so this was not a new scenario.

Ronald Shephard argued that the reopening of the Southwold Railway '...would help the war effort and assist the financial recovery of Southwold after the war'. But, as the history books show, the scheme came to naught. The Southwold Railway did not reopen in any guise, let alone as a standard gauge line worked by a Sentinel locomotive hired from the LNER. The foregoing is, therefore, merely a 'what might have been'. But it is rather interesting to imagine how things would have looked and worked. One for creative modellers, perhaps?

Note: Much of the foregoing is based on A Memorandum on the Southwold Railway, *an address made by Ronald Shephard in 1941. A copy of the document was kindly made available to us by Mr.Derek Clayton. Many thanks, Derek!*

2-4-0T No.3 BLYTH runs round its train at Halesworth in 1911. The GER station is on the left. The signals are typical Southwold in that up and down signals are on the same post. PHOTOGRAPH: ERIC ASHTON COLLECTION

No.3 BLYTH at Blythburgh *circa* 1920. Milk churns await collection on the platform. To the left, there seems to be ample siding accommodation for such a small wayside station. PHOTOGRAPH: ERIC ASHTON COLLECTION

PHILADELPHIA —

the later years

Just before World War I the nation's coal output peaked at 287,000,000 tons per year. Since then the industry has been in decline. For many years the decline was very slow but by the mid-1940s – particularly after the difficulties of the war years – the industry was in a distinctly parlous state. The Government's answer was the nationalisation of the coal industry. This was effected on 1 January 1947.

The newly-created National Coal Board put in hand a programme of modernisation and improvements in the coalfields, and the industry made a partial recovery in the 1950s. However, by the early 1960s the ever-increasing competition from oil, in particular, had brought a renewed uncertainty to the industry and this led, somewhat inevitably, to contraction and closures. One of the casualties of the period was Lambton Staiths on the River Wear. The staiths closed on 5 January 1967, and this brought an end to the practice of NCB locomotives working on 4¾ miles of British Railways metals from Penshaw to Sunderland.

Lambton Staiths were an outlet for collieries which, in pre-NCB days, had

> ### by Brian Syddall
> **with additional material**
> **by Colin E. Mountford**

been part of the Lambton Hetton & Joicey empire. The colliery company had had an extensive railway system, the locomotive and engineering headquarters of which were at Philadelphia, some six miles south-west of Sunderland. The Philadelphia complex included four engine sheds, the well-known Lambton Engine Works and a wagon works, and at one time it even had its own electricity generating station. In later years Philadelphia was a major draw for railway enthusiasts but, before seeing why, here's the history bit...

Background
The complex history of railways here goes back some 200 years to the days of the wagonways which were used to transport coal to loading points on the River Wear. The early wagonways were, of course, horse-worked and/or rope-worked, but in 1814 a steam locomotive was tried on the Newbottle Waggonway. This machine was assembled at Newbottle Colliery in October 1814 and, before long, was rebuilt with a new boiler. However, the new boiler exploded in July 1815 and the locomotive was apparently dumped alongside the track. Another locomotive – an eight-

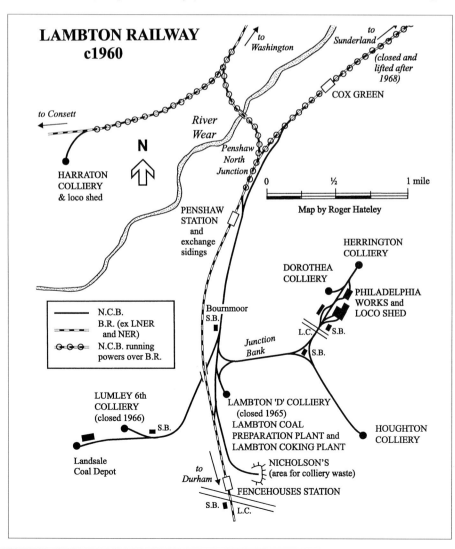

LAMBTON RAILWAY c1960

to Washington

to Sunderland

(closed and lifted after 1968)

COX GREEN

to Consett

River Wear

Penshaw North Junction

N

0   ½   1 mile

Map by Roger Hateley

HARRATON COLLIERY & loco shed

PENSHAW STATION and exchange sidings

HERRINGTON COLLIERY

DOROTHEA COLLIERY

PHILADELPHIA WORKS and LOCO SHED

Bournmoor S.B.

L.C.   S.B.

Junction Bank

S.B.

— N.C.B.
--- B.R. (ex LNER and NER)
–o–o–o– N.C.B. running powers over B.R.

LUMLEY 6th COLLIERY *(closed 1966)*

S.B.

Landsale Coal Depot

LAMBTON 'D' COLLIERY *(closed 1965)*
LAMBTON COAL PREPARATION PLANT and LAMBTON COKING PLANT

HOUGHTON COLLIERY

to Durham

NICHOLSON'S *(area for colliery waste)*

FENCEHOUSES STATION

S.B.   L.C.

wheeled machine – was tested on the Lambton Waggonway in December 1814 and is believed to have remained there, still on test, until the following year.

The owner of the Lambton Waggonway – and one of the principal figures in the local coal industry – was John George Lambton (who became Baron Durham in 1828 and the Earl of Durham in 1833). In July 1822 he purchased at auction the Newbottle Waggonway and extended it to join the Lambton Waggonway. As additional pits were sunk the wagonway system was extended accordingly and some of the older sections were either improved or, in many cases, replaced by new lines. By 1840 the Lambton system comprised over 40 route miles, all of which was worked by horses, ropes or stationary engines.

The transition to locomotive working started in 1852. The York Newcastle & Berwick (later NER) branch from Penshaw to Sunderland opened in December of that year and, significantly, the Earl of Durham (as he then was) had running powers over the branch. By using a connection between the Lambton lines and the YNB a little to the east of Millfield station, the Earl was able to run

a celebrated NCB depot

locomotive-hauled trains to the staiths – he no longer had to run all of his traffic over his own rope-worked system. In October 1865 the NER opened its goods branch to Deptford on the River Wear; the Earl of Durham had a ¼-mile long branch of his own built from this line via a narrow double-track tunnel direct to Lambton Staiths. The Earl also obtained running powers to Sunderland's South Dock (which had opened in 1850) and over the NER's Pontop & Shields branch as far as

An industrial on the main line... The date is 27 August 1965, and Robert Stephenson 0-6-2T No.10 approaches Cox Green station on the BR line with a lengthy train of coal from Herrington Colliery to Sunderland Staiths. Note the wooden hopper wagons – even in the mid-1960s they were still popular with the NCB in the north-east, particularly on staiths work. Prior to *circa* 1930 there were two additional tracks to the left of the lines seen here; these were for Lambton traffic only – they joined the 'main line' on the far side of the level crossing. In this picture, all trace of the junction (Cox Green Junction) seems to have vanished. The signal box behind No.10 was installed *circa* 1930 as part of the new arrangements; it replaced the old Cox Green Junction box. **PHOTOGRAPH: IAN S.CARR**

STAITHS in SUNDERLAND c1960

to Newcastle

N

Deptford Branch

Hetton Staiths

SOUTH DOCK

to Penshaw

PALLION

MILLFIELD

Lambton Staiths

SUNDERLAND

[Original Lambton Railway]

Fawcett St. Jct.

[Original Hetton Railway]

to Seaham & Durham, etc.

BR (ex LNER & NER)
NCB
NCB running powers over BR

0   ½   1 mile

Map by Roger Hateley

Harraton Colliery, Lambton trains having to reverse at Penshaw North Junction. These running powers were extended to North Biddick Colliery when the Earl acquired it in 1894. And so, with these various running powers, the Earl of Durham finished up with a useful choice of routes by which his coal could be dispatched for shipment. Nevertheless, as the output from the Earl of Durham's

One of the distinctive sights at Philadelphia was the magnificent coaling gantry. On an unspecified date in 1952 Robert Stephenson 0-6-2T No.5 stands adjacent to the coaling road. The engine is painted in the first NCB livery of medium green with black lining and white edges, yellow lettering, and red rods and buffer beams. And what a picture it is too! No.5 is one of four ex-Lambton steamers to have been saved for preservation; it now lives on the North York Moors Railway. The buildings in the background on the right, incidentally, are part of Dorothea Colliery. PHOTOGRAPH: J.DAWSON; A.R.THOMPSON COLLECTION

collieries increased, the amount of traffic using the NER lines also increased, and to help ease the flow of traffic at Penshaw the Earl of Durham laid a pair of lines parallel to the NER lines between Penshaw North and Cox Green station. The Earl of Durham's lines joined the NER lines immediately to the south of Cox Green station (the junction being logically known as Cox Green Junction), thereby enabling the Lambton traffic to avoid Penshaw North Junction. However, the arrangements were altered *circa* 1930 when the junction between the Lambton lines and the ex-NER lines reverted to Penshaw North, the two independent mineral lines between there and Cox Green being removed.

Going back to the 1890s, by this time the Earl of Durham was not in the best of financial health and could not afford to undertake the modernisation which his collieries needed. He therefore sold his business to Sir James Joicey, another prominent local colliery owner in County Durham. The sale was made in 1896, and Joicey set up a company titled Lambton Collieries Ltd to administer the acquisitions.

In August 1911 the Lambton company absorbed the Hetton Coal Company to form the Lambton & Hetton Collieries Ltd. The Hetton company had an eight-mile long railway to its own staiths on

the River Wear (this railway had been engineered by George Stephenson) and, following the amalgamation of the two companies, the Hetton and the Lambton railways were physically connected by means of a tunnel linking the two sets of staiths. In November 1924 the Lambton & Hetton company took over James Joicey & Co to form The Lambton, Hetton & Joicey Collieries Ltd.

This new conglomerate was the largest of the Durham colliery companies. It controlled a substantial group of coal railways, with the Lambton system being the busiest and most extensive of them all.

Lambton Engine Works
As mentioned earlier, the locomotive and engineering headquarters of the Lambton system were at Philadelphia. A 'Philadelphia Yard' is shown on a plan dated 1835, and this is clearly the embryo of what became the Lambton Engine Works. As the Lambton empire expanded and the railway system gradually embraced locomotive working, the workshops had to cope with a wider range of tasks. It was therefore eventually decided that additional facilities would be desirable and, in 1882, a brand new fitting and erecting shop was brought into use. Although the original premises had latterly become somewhat cramped, an

impressive range of jobs had been carried out there and, in 1877, the works had even built an 0-6-0 tender engine.

The new, expanded, workshop complex came to be known as the Lambton Engine Works. The new fitting shop itself was a tall, airy building 210 feet by 75 feet wide and with double gable ends, one of which housed a large clock overlooking the works yard. In 1883 it was equipped with a 30-ton overhead crane which had been made by the Grange Iron Works near Belmont. The other side of the building served as a machine and fitting shop. In addition, a small boiler shop was situated adjacent to the main building.

When the Lambton company amalgamated with the Hetton Coal Company in 1911 the latter brought into the fold its own workshops. The former Hetton premises were closed during the winter of 1934/35, all locomotive work subsequently being dealt with at Philadelphia. The Philadelphia works could handle up to seven locomotive repairs at one time, although in later years four become the more usual number. The workforce was usually split into two gangs, each under the supervision of a chargehand, with two locomotives allocated to each gang. During the course of a year, around eighteen to twenty locomotives were dealt with at the works.

The Lambton Engine Works was

Above. Another view of the Philadelphia coaling gantry (note the two chutes), this time looking in a south-westerly direction towards one of the engine sheds. The engine is Vulcan Foundry-built 'Austerity' No.58; it had come to the Lambton system in 1946 and remained until the end of steam working in 1969, after which it was transferred to Derwenthaugh. It was scrapped at Derwenthaugh in October 1972. This angle gives a good view of No.58's rounded cab roof. This was a feature of many Lambton engines as, if they were employed on 'main line' runs or duties at the staiths on the River Wear, they had to be able to negotiate the tight bore of the tunnel from the Deptford branch to the staiths. PHOTOGRAPH: V.WAKE; COURTESY THE ARMSTRONG TRUST

Below. The heart of the Philadelphia complex was the Lambton Engine Works. This fine view was taken from the gantry at the south-west end of the erecting shop; the engines under repair are standing, as was the custom, on the track which ran the full length of the north-west wall. The wrought iron overhead crane in the top right-hand corner of the picture was made by the Grange Iron Works near Belmont in 1883 and, after the closure of the Lambton Engine Works in 1989, it was rescued by the Bowes Railway. This picture was taken on 17 July 1968 while No.5 was in the throes of its final overhaul under NCB ownership. PHOTOGRAPH: IAN S.CARR

The running line at Philadelphia crossed the A182 Shiney Row-Houghton le Spring road on the level. For most visitors, this was the first view of the Philadelphia complex and the first helping of the atmosphere there. One of the engine sheds can be seen in mid-distance on the far side of the running lines – the other sheds and the Lambton Engine works are over to the right, out of view. Although the houses still remain, the imposing box next to the crossing has now gone. PHOTOGRAPH: IAN S.CARR

almost completely self-sufficient and at least three 0-6-0 tender engines were built there – one in 1877, another in 1890 and the third in 1894. Until *circa* 1906 the works also made some of its own locomotive boilers. The works undertook a very wide range of tasks – besides all the engineering work for the locomotives and collieries it also maintained the company's large fleet of ships, while at the other end of the scale it handled the leather straps used for pit pony harnesses. The works had its own iron and brass foundries (which lasted until the 1980s) and originally had its own rolling mills as well.

As for the Lambton-built locomotives, the use of 0-6-0 tender engines on a colliery railway might seem unusual but, as the Lambton company had running powers over certain NER lines (as was discussed earlier), some 'main line' running was required. Over the years, the Lambton company and its successors owned no less than twenty-two 0-6-0 tender engines. Most came from Hudswell & Clarke (as the firm was titled until 1870) or Robert Stephenson, but a couple of lesser-known builders were also represented: Thomas Richardson of the Castle Eden Foundry at Hartlepool supplied two 0-6-0s while John Coulthard & Co of Quarry Field Works at Gateshead supplied three. It has been suggested elsewhere that the Coulthard locomotives were actually built by Robert Stephenson & Co, Coulthard merely acting as an agent, but there is no evidence to support this suggestion.

After the nationalisation of the coal industry on 1 January 1947, the Lambton Railway became part of the National Coal Board's Northern Division No.2 Area (Mid-East Durham) and the Lambton Engine Works became the central workshops for that area.

The generating station
In 1905 the Lambton & Hetton company started to construct its own electricity generating station at Philadelphia. The station was taken over by the Newcastle-upon-Tyne Electric Supply Co on 1 April 1907 – this was either before, or as, it became operational. It supplied the workshops and various colliery installations.

In May 1908 the Newcastle-upon-Tyne Electric Supply Co took over the power station's distribution system, and in October 1913 took over the *whole* of the Lambton company's distribution system.

The power station was served by sidings from the Engine Works complex, the shunting of the sidings being performed by Lambton & Hetton locomotives. In 1918 a four-wheeled battery electric locomotive was purchased from Dick Kerr for shunting at the generating station and, despite the fact that the station was owned by the Newcastle-upon-Tyne company, in 1925 the electric locomotive was added to Lambton Hetton & Joicey stock as their No.51. This locomotive had its own shed at Phildelphia. The generating station closed in 1936 and the battery-electric locomotive was scrapped soon after.

Philadelphia sheds
There had once been various engine sheds serving different components of the Lambton Hetton & Joicey empire but, by the time of nationalisation in January 1947, the only ones remaining on the former LH&J system were those at Philadelphia, at Lambton Staiths and at the north end of the old Hetton Railway. The Philadelphia sheds were close to Lambton Engine Works at Philadelphia and, as we have already seen, there were four separate buildings (though one of the four was latterly used for washing out and another was ultimately used to store engines).

The main engine shed, built in 1917 and situated on the other side of the main line, had two roads holding about eight tank engines, with a high level coaling ramp and delivery shutes running along the shed yard. It was a very convenient arrangement and 'top of the range' compared with the usual industrial railway coaling facilities. It even put many British Railways MPDs to shame!

On Vesting Day there were at least fifty-four locomotives employed on the old Lambton system. Of these, eight were at Lambton Staiths shed (a large two-road building situated alongside the landward edge of the system), four were at Hetton shed and one was at Harraton Colliery. The other forty-three were all based at Philadelphia. It is probable that another engine (No.37) was also at Philadelphia on Vesting Day – this engine is known to have been at Handen Hold Colliery, but it is very likely that it had returned to

Kitson 0-6-2T No.29 is being prepared for work while 0-6-0ST No.58 trundles past light engine on one of the running lines. The ascending line on the left goes to the coaling gantry while, on the right, various worshop buildings can be seen on the other side of the running lines. The date is 3 January 1969. PHOTOGRAPH: IAN S.CARR

Philadelphia before January 1947. Twelve of the Philadelphia engines were 0-6-2Ts; the others were a mix of 0-6-0 and 0-4-0 tender and tank engines, some of which were of considerable vintage. Up to ten of the engines could be found working each day between Herrington and Houghton Collieries, Lambton Coke Works and Penshaw exchange sidings. The Philadelphia engines were highly distinctive in that they had cut-down cabs, this being due to the restricted clearances through the tunnel on the Deptford branch.

0-6-2Ts – new and old

We have already mentioned the Lambton Railway's 0-6-2Ts. The first of these was purchased new from Kitson's in 1904; two more were obtained from Kitson's in 1907, two from Robert Stephenson's in 1909 and another from Robert Stephenson in 1920. Up to this time almost all of the Lambton locomotives (including those inherited from the Hetton Coal Company) had been purchased new, but between 1929 and 1931 five 0-6-2Ts were purchased from the Great Western Railway. Given that the Lambton's earlier 0-6-2Ts had become highly regarded, the company was no doubt pleased to pick up engines of a vaguely similar type for a bargain price.

Although the five second-hand 0-6-2Ts were purchased from the GWR, they had not started their lives with that company.

They had been acquired by the GWR at the Grouping – two had come from the Cardiff Railway and three had belonged to the Taff Vale Railway. In South Wales they had proved to be versatile machines, ideal for the heavy coal traffic in the valleys, but in 1924 the GWR had introduced its own up-to-date 0-6-2Ts (the 56XXs) and, soon after, the South Wales coal traffic entered a period of decline. These factors had rendered many of the older pre-grouping engines redundant. Many were scrapped, but some were sold for use elsewhere.

The five ex-GWR 0-6-2Ts were purchased via the agents R.H.Longbotham & Co; they were:
• GWR No.426; Taff Vale 'O2' class (TVR

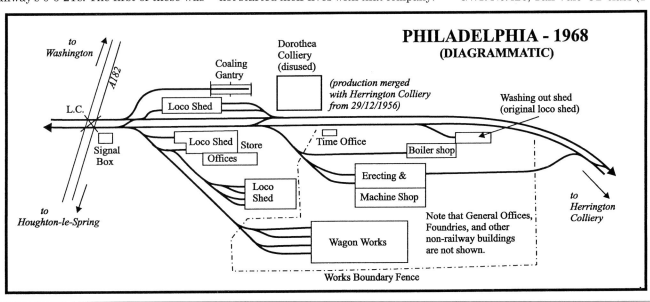

PHILADELPHIA - 1968 (DIAGRAMMATIC)

to Washington

A182

L.C.

Signal Box

to Houghton-le-Spring

Coaling Gantry

Loco Shed

Loco Shed | Store

Offices

Loco Shed

Dorothea Colliery (disused)

(production merged with Herrington Colliery from 29/12/1956)

Time Office

Erecting & Machine Shop

Wagon Works

Boiler shop

Washing out shed (original loco shed)

to Herrington Colliery

Note that General Offices, Foundries, and other non-railway buildings are not shown.

Works Boundary Fence

NCB LOCOMOTIVES USED ON THE FORMER LAMBTON HETTON & JOICEY SYSTEM, 1947 UNTIL CLOSURE (listed in order of arrival)

Makers abbreviated thus: AB – Andrew Barclay; **BH** – Black Hawthorn; **BP** – Beyer Peacock; **Dar** – BR Darlington; **Der** – BR Derby; **ED** – Earl of Durham; **EE** – English Electric; **GR** – Grant Richie; **H&C** – Hudswell & Clarke; **HCR** – Hudswell Clarke & Rogers; **HL** – Hawthorn Leslie; **JC** – John Coulthard; **K** – Kitson; **KS** – Kerr Stuart; **LEW** – Lambton Engine Works; **MW** – Manning Wardle; **NB** – North British Locomotive Co (Queens Park Works); **P** – Peckett; **NR** – Neilson Reid; **RR** – Rolls Royce; **RS** – Robert Stephenson; **RSH** – Robert Stephenson & Hawthorns; **RWH** – R&W Hawthorn; **S** – Sentinel; **SN** – BR Swindon; **TV** – Taff Vale Railway (Cardiff); **VF** – Vulcan Foundry

N.B: In a number of cases locomotives had been withdrawn from service a few years before they were scrapped ¶

NCB No.	Type	Built	Maker; W/No.	Wheels	Cylinders; h.p.	To Lambton	Scrapped ¶ or transferred	Disposal
1	0-6-0	1866	H&C 71	4' 0"	17" x 24" (i)	New	8.1954	Scrapped
3	0-6-0	1865	BP 550	4' 6"	17" x 24" (i)	New	10.1954	Scrapped
4	0-6-0	1866	BH 17	4' 6"	16½" x 24 " (i)	New	10.1954	Scrapped
5	0-6-2T	1909	RS 3377	4' 6"	18½" x 26" (i)	New	8.1970	Preserved (see text)
6	0-6-0	c.1853	JC -	4' 6"	16" x 24 " (i)	?	1951	Scrapped
7	0-6-0	c.1853	JC -	4' 6"	16" x 24 " (i)	?	c.3.1952	Scrapped †
8	0-6-0	c.1853	JC -	4' 6"	16" x 24 " (i)	?	c.3.1952	Scrapped
9	0-6-0	1877	ED -	4' 6"	17" x 24" (i)	New	9.1962 #	Retained as stationary boiler at Philadelphia; transferred to Brancepeth Colliery 1962
10	0-6-2T	1909	RS 3378	4' 6"	18½" x 26" (i)	New	1.1969	Scrapped
11	0-4-0ST	1920	HC 1412	3' 9"	16" x 24" (o)	New	3.1969	Transferred to Hylton Colliery
12	0-4-0ST	1912	HL 2789	3' 10"	16" x 24" (o)	New	1960	Transferred to Dawdon Colliery
13	0-4-0ST	1914	HL 3055	3' 10"	16" x 24" (o)	New	8.1961	Transferred to Vane Tempest Colliery
14	0-4-0ST	1914	HL 3056	3' 10"	16" x 24" (o)	New	11.1962	To Dawdon Colliery; (later preserved)
15	0-4-0ST	1875	HCR 169	3' 7"	15" x 20" (o)	New	2.1952	Scrapped
16	0-4-0ST	1870	H&C 96	3' 7"	15" x 20" (o)	New	2.1952	Scrapped
17	0-4-0ST	1923	MW 2023	3' 9"	15" x 22" (o)	New	8.1960	Scrapped
18	0-6-0ST*	1867*	BH 32*	4' 0"	15" x 20" (o)	New	2.1960	Sold to the Seaham Harbour Dock Co
19	0-4-0ST	1871	MW 344	3' 0"	12" x 18" (o)	New	11.1947	Transferred to South Hetton Colliery
20	0-6-0	1876	RS 2260	4' 6"	17" x 24" (i)	New	c.8.1960	Scrapped
21	0-4-0ST	1876	RS 2308	3' 7"	15" x 20" (o)	New	1954	Scrapped
22	0-4-0ST	1881	HC 230	3' 7"	15" x 20" (o)	New	c.6.1958	Scrapped
23	0-4-0ST	1882	BH 688	3' 7"	15 x 20 (i)	New	1.1963	Scrapped
24	0-4-0ST	1885	BH 832	3' 7"	15 x 20 (i)	New	9.1957 **	Scrapped **
25	0-6-0	1890	ED -	4' 6"	17" x 24" (i)	New	5.1960	Scrapped
26	0-6-0	1894	ED -	4' 6"	17" x 24" (i)	New	12.1962	Scrapped
27	0-6-0ST*	1845*	RS 491	5' 8"	14" x 22" (o)	1898	11.1968	Scrapped
28	0-4-0ST	1902	HL 2530	3' 6"	14" x 20" (o)	New	10.1968	Scrapped
29	0-6-2T	1904	K 4263	4' 6"	19" x 26" (i)	New	7.1970	Preserved (see text)
30	0-6-2T	1907	K 4532	4' 6"	19" x 26" (i)	New	1.1969	Scrapped
31	0-6-2T	1907	K 4533	4' 6"	19" x 26" (i)	New	11.1968	Scrapped
32	0-4-0ST	1910	HL 2826	3' 8"	15" x 22" (o)	New	8.1967	Scrapped
33	0-4-0ST	1910	HL 2827	3' 8"	15" x 22" (o)	New	10.1968	Scrapped
34	0-4-0ST	1912	HL 2954	3' 8"	15" x 22" (o)	New	12.1966	Transferred to Silksworth Colliery
35	0-4-0ST	1913	HL 3024	3' 8"	15" x 22" (o)	New	7.1966	Transferred to Silksworth Colliery
36 ††	0-4-0ST	1896	P 615	3' 3¾"	14" x 20" (o)	1919 ‡‡	1.1963	Scrapped
37	0-6-0ST	1868	RWH 1430	3' 6"	15" x 22" (i)	1919 ‡‡	1951	Scrapped
39	0-6-0ST	1867	RWH 1422	3' 6"	15½" x 22" (i)	1919 ‡‡	1951	Scrapped †
41	0-6-0T	1917	KS 3074	4' 0"	17" x 24" (i)	c.1920	10.1964	Scrapped
42	0-6-2T	1920	RS 3801	4' 6"	18½" x 26" (i)	New	5.1970	Scrapped
43	0-4-0ST	1920	GR 769	3' 7"	16" x 24" (o)	New	5.1961	Transferred to Seaham Colliery
44	0-6-0T*	1917*	MW 1934	3' 9"	17" x 24" (o)	New	2.1960	Sold to the Seaham Harbour Dock Co
45	0-6-0ST	1912	HL 2932	3' 9"	15" x 22" (o)	1920	12.1970	Scrapped
46	0-6-0T	1913	MW 1813	4' 2"	18" x 24" (i)	1920	4.1960	Scrapped
47	0-4-0ST	1923	HL 3543	3' 8"	15" x 22" (o)	New	c.12.1968	Transferred to Hylton Colliery
48	0-4-0ST	1923	HL 3544	3' 8"	15" x 22" (o)	New	4.1965	Transferred to Seaham Colliery
49	0-4-0ST	1924	MW 2035	3' 9"	15" x 22" (o)	New	5.1964	Transferred to Dawdon Colliery
50	0-4-0ST	1924	MW 2036 **	3' 9"	15" x 22" (o)	New **	11.1958	Transferred to Vane Tempest Colliery
52	0-6-2T	1899	NR 5408	4' 6½"	17½" x 26" (i)	1929	2.1971	Preserved (see text)
53	0-6-2T	1894	TV 302	4' 6½"	17½" x 26" (i)	1930	10.1966	Scrapped
54	0-6-2T	1897	TV 311	4' 6½"	17½" x 26" (i)	1930	9.1958	Scrapped
55	0-6-2T	1887	K 3069	4' 6"	17½" x 26" (i)	1931	c.8.1961	Scrapped
56	0-6-2T	1894	K 3580	4' 6"	17½" x 26" (i)	1931	1.1954	Scrapped
57	0-6-2T	1934	HL 3834	4' 6"	18½" x 26" (i)	New	5.1964	Scrapped
58	0-6-0ST	1945	VF 5299	4' 3"	18" x 26" (i)	1946	3.1969	Transferred to Derwenthaugh
59	0-6-0ST	1945	VF 5300	4' 3"	18" x 26" (i)	1946	3.1969	Transferred to Derwenthaugh
60	0-6-0ST	1948	HE 3686	4' 3"	18" x 26" (i)	New	7.1965	Transferred to Dawdon Colliery
No.2	0-6-0ST	1949	RSH 7599	3' 8"	16" x 24" (o)	New	2.1970	Scrapped
No.37	0-4-0ST	1953	RSH 7755	3' 8"	15" x 22" (o)	New	1.1967	Transferred to Dawdon Colliery
No.38	0-4-0ST	1953	RSH 7756	3' 8"	15" x 22" (o)	New	7.1965	Transferred to Seaham Colliery
No.39	0-6-0ST	1953	RSH 7757	3' 8"	15" x 22" (o)	New	3.1967	Transferred to Wearmouth Colliery
7	0-6-0ST	1954	HE 3820	4' 3"	18" x 26" (i)	New	3.1969	Transferred to Derwenthaugh

continued opposite...

No.85), built by Neilson Reid (W/ No.5408) in May 1899. Withdrawn January 1927; sold April 1929. **Became LH&J No.52**

• GWR No.448; Taff Vale 'O' class (TVR No.26), built at the TVR's works at Cardiff West Yard in November 1894. Sold direct from running stock in February 1930. **Became LH&J No.53**

• GWR No.475; Taff Vale 'O1' class (TVR No.64), built at the TVR's works at Cardiff West Yard in October 1897. Sold direct from running stock in February 1930. **Became LH&J No.54**

• GWR No.159; ex-Cardiff Railway (CR No.28), built by Kitson & Co (W/No.3069) in 1887. Sold direct from running stock in February 1931. **Became LH&J No.55**

• GWR No.156; ex-Cardiff Railway (CR No.1), built by Kitson & Co (W/No.3580) in 1894. Sold direct from running stock in February 1931. **Became LH&J No.56**

The ex-GWR engines were used on the Philadelphia-Penshaw-Sunderland run and also on the Hetton line between North Moor and Lambton Staithes.

There was little doubt that the Lambton company favoured the 0-6-2T format as in 1934 a brand new example – the company's twelfth 0-6-2T – was purchased from Hawthorn Leslie. All twelve passed to the NCB in 1947. They

became known locally as the 'mainliners' as they took over from the 0-6-0s on the runs to Sunderland.

Rebuildings

In the early 1950s the works manager at Philadelphia, Mr.T.W.Lawson, a former pupil of Sir Nigel Gresley, and something of a steam enthusiast himself, put in hand a number of rebuilds and improvements to the hard-worked locomotives of that time. It was perhaps part of the NCB modernisation plan, at a time when maximum production was called for, in the days before the advent of alternative fuels.

...continued from opposite

1	0-6-0DH	1955	NB 27410	3' 6"	400 hp	New	1.1968	Transferred to Wearmouth Colliery
51 ¢	0-6-0ST	1943	RSH 7101	4' 3"	18" x 26" (i)	12.1955 ¢	8.1969	Transferred to Morrison Busty Colliery
6	0-6-0PT	1958	LEW -	4' 7"	16" x 24" (i)	New	10.1964	Scrapped
No.63	0-6-0ST	1949	RSH 7600	3' 8"	16" x 24" (o)	11.1958	5.1970	Scrapped
85 ‡	0-6-0ST	1935	RS 4113	3' 10"	16" x 24" (o)	8.1960	1.1964	Scrapped
-	4w DM	1957	FH 3852	3' 1½"	75hp	1962	9.1965	Transferred to Hylton Colliery
3	0-6-0ST	1951	RSH 7687	4' 0"	18" x 24" (o)	1.1963	10.1968	Scrapped
4	0-6-0ST	1951	RSH 7688	4' 0"	18" x 24" (o)	1.1963	12.1968	Scrapped
8	0-6-0ST	1951	RSH 7691	4' 0"	18" x 24" (o)	1.1963	3.1970	Scrapped
506	0-6-0DH	1964	SN (D9504)	4' 0"	650 hp	11.1968	8.1973	To Boldon Colliery; (later preserved)
507	0-6-0DH	1965	SN (D9525)	4' 0"	650 hp	11.1968	3.1975	Transferred to Burradon Colliery
508	0-6-0DH	1965	SN (D9540)	4' 0"	650 hp	11.1968	11.1971	Transferred to Burradon Colliery
506 ##	0-6-0DH	1965	HE 6617	3' 8"	311 hp	2.1969	4.1971	Transferred to Derwenthaugh
509	0-6-0DE	1952	Dar (12119)	4' 0½"	350 hp	2.1969	11.1985	Scrapped
510	0-6-0DE	1952	Dar (12120)	4' 0½"	350 hp	2.1969	3.1980	Scrapped
511	0-6-0DE	1952	Dar (12133)	4' 0½"	350 hp	5.1969	11.1985	Scrapped
512	0-6-0DE	1949	Der (12060)	4' 0½"	350 hp	4.1971	12.1985	Scrapped
513	0-6-0DE	1952	Der (12098)	4' 0½"	350 hp	4.1971	9.1985	Sold to National Smokeless Fuels; (pres.)
514	0-6-0DE	1950	Der (12084)	4' 0½"	350 hp	11.1971	4.1972 +	Transferred to Hylton Colliery +
No.52	0-6-0DE	1961	Dar (D4070)	4' 6"	350 hp	9.1976	11.1976	Transferred to Bates Colliery
9101/66	0-6-0DH	1966	HE 6662	3' 9"	311 hp	5.1977	3.1978	Transferred to Derwenthaugh
-	0-4-0DH	1964	RR 10201	3' 6"	325 hp	4.1977	5.1979	Transferred to Seaham Colliery
101	4w DM	1959	FH 3922	3' 0"	134 hp	4.1977	8.1979	Preserved (see text)
9101/65	0-6-0DH	1966	EE D1121	?	305 hp	7.1979	1980	Scrapped
-	0-6-0DH	1979	AB 647	3' 9"	400 hp	New	6.1980	Transferred to South Hetton Colliery
2100/522	0-6-0DH	1973	AB 585	3' 9"	400 hp	9.1981	5.1983	Transferred to Bates Colliery
No.53	0-6-0DE	1961	Dar (D4072)	4' 6"	350 hp	10.1981	6.1982	Transferred to South Hetton Colliery
20/110/705	0-6-0DH	1976	AB 604	3' 9"	400 hp	6.1982	9.1982	Transferred to South Hetton Colliery
D3088	0-6-0DE	1954	Der -	4' 6"	350 hp	11.1982	2.1983	Transferred to Bates Colliery
-	0-4-0DH	1967	AB 523	3' 9"	233 hp	12.1982	3.1983	Transferred to Seaham Colliery

* No.18 originally an 0-6-0 but later rebuilt as 0-6-0ST
† Parts of Nos.7, 8 and 39 incorporated in the 'new' No.6
No.27 originally an 0-6-0ST; rebuilt as an 0-6-0T at the Lambton Engine Works 1904
No.44 originally an 0-6-0ST; rebuilt as an 0-6-0T in 1951
†† No.36 originally named HAZARD, may later have run as NORTH HETTON No.1, but no name carried as a Lambton engine
‡‡ Ex-North Hetton Coal Co, taken over as part of the Lambton and Hetton merger in 1911 (No.36 not renumbered in LHJ stock until 1919)
‡ No.85 named VANE TEMPEST
# To Brancepeth Colliery 2.1962 and scrapped there 8.1965
** No.50 rebuilt at Lambton Engine Works 1956/57; boiler off No.24 used for the 'new' no.50; (No.24 had had boiler removed by 1956 but was not formally withdrawn until 9.1957)
¢ Purchased by the NCB in 1947 for use as the Divisional spare loco and was at first numbered 60; renumbered 51 by 3.1949; worked at various places in Northumberland and Durham but was not regularly employed on the Lambton system until 12.1955
No.506 renumbered 209 in 8.1969
+ Returned to Philadelphia 10.1983 as a source of spares; scrapped 11.1985

Worthy of mention are the tender cabs fitted to 0-6-0s Nos. 9 and 26 – these locomotives had been built at Philadelphia in 1877 and 1894 respectively. Also of note was the rebuilding in 1951 of No.44, a Manning Wardle outside-cylindered 0-6-0ST (W/No.1934 of 1917) which, it was thought, would benefit from a 'modern' look. The saddle tank was replaced by side tanks; what looked like a taper boiler and Belpaire firebox was achieved only by the shape of the outer clothing (or cladding). The result was rather odd, not being helped by the lack of a dome and the squat, cut-down cab. This strange looking machine was sold to the Seaham Harbour and Dock Company in 1960. It did not last long there – it was scrapped in July 1963.

Another rebuild in the fullest sense of the word was seen in 1958 when an inside-cylindered 0-6-0 pannier tank (No.6) was constructed from parts of three withdrawn locomotives – veteran 0-6-0s Nos.6 and 7 and 0-6-0ST No.39. The resulting machine had full-length pannier tanks with a camber in line with the cut back cab, while the front of the tanks was supported by the sandboxes on top of the platform. This, the last of the conversions and perhaps being none too successful, was scrapped in 1964.

A routine job at the Engine Works was repainting. In LH&JC days the locomotives were very attractively turned out in a medium green livery, with black lining edged with white, red side rods and

buffer beams, with the initials LHJC in gold, shaded red, on the side tanks. Under the Coal Board's command, this livery was progressively reduced. First the words National Coal Board were reduced to just the initials and the lining was simplified – in the 1960s plain green was used, followed by glossy black. However, when fresh from overhaul they still looked smart with buffer beams and coupling rods in red, and yellow for the lettering and numbers.

My visits

In the 1960s there was a great deal to see in the industrial railway field, but there was so little time. However, news of an impending closure invariably resulted in time somehow 'being found' for a visit to the relevant site. In the case of the Philadelphia system, I missed the last days of the Lambton Staiths (they closed on 5 January 1967), so I made sure that I paid a visit to Philadelphia before any further closures took place. And, as it transpired, it couldn't have been left much later.

By the time of my first visit in 1968, even with the loss of the Sunderland workings, the Lambton Railways was still a fascinating system with plenty of photographic opportunities. As a bonus, there was also the possibility of one or two locomotives in for overhaul from other collieries in the Durham area.

My first visit was, in fact, on 24 February 1968. Getting there was a relatively simple matter – British

Railways to Sunderland, followed by a bus ride on Sunderland District's service No.39 from the bus station, alighting at the level crossing gates at Philadelphia. I was then confronted with an array of buildings apparently of Victorian vintage, with engine sheds on both sides of the fully signalled double track, the signal box, impressive coaling ramp and, in the background, Lambton Engine works and the winding gear of the closed Dorothea Colliery.

By 1968 I was a little too late to see some of the more exotic members of the old Lambton fleet. Among those I missed were the 0-6-0 tender engines. No less than ten of these – including three which had been built at Philadelphia – had survived to be taken into NCB stock in 1947, but six of the ten had been scrapped in the first half of the 1950s, two had been scrapped in 1960, and the final pair had gone (one to Brancepeth Colliery, the other for scrap) in 1962.

Nevertheless, at the time of my visit there was one remarkable veteran – nominally, at least. This was No.27 which was reputed to have been built by Robert Stephenson as a 2-4-0 for the Newcastle & Darlington Junction Railway in 1845 (W/No.491). In 1864 it was rebuilt at the NER's Gateshead Works as an 0-6-0 and in 1873 was rebuilt with a saddle tank before being sold to the Lambton company in 1898. It was rebuilt yet again at Lambton Engine Works in 1904, emerging this time with side tanks. A popular engine, notwithstanding its limited coal

RSH 0-6-0ST No.8 drifts past Philadelphia sheds with a heavy load of coal from Herrington Colliery. No.8 came to Philadelphia in January 1963, having previously been with Dorman Long at Lackenby. It was scrapped at Philadelphia in 1970. The winding gear on the left of the picture is that of Dorothea Colliery; this pit merged with Herrington as from the beginning of 1957. PHOTOGRAPH: IAN S.CARR

capacity, it managed to survive until December 1968, by which time it was 123 years of age. That said, very little, if anything, could have remained of the original machine.

When I visited Philadelphia in 1968 the 'main line' workings were shared between the last two working 0-6-2Ts, Nos.5 and 29, and one of that classic industrial type, Austerity 0-6-0ST No.58,

one of three of this class allocated here at the time. Shunting at the two remaining collieries, Lambton Coke Works and the Washer was carried out by the smaller engines.

After steam working ceased on the Lambton system in 1969 a handful of locomotives were placed in store in the crumbling four-road engine shed at Philadelphia. On 6 June 1970 the occupants were No.29 and No.5 (left-hand road) and No.52, one of the erstwhile GWR 0-6-2Ts (right-hand road). All three of these engines were saved for preservation. The brake van at the far end of the shed appears to have been Lambton designed and built. It is a relic of the days when Lambton/NCB trains used to run over BR metals to Sunderland. PHOTOGRAPH: IAN S.CARR

Loco roster at Philadelphia, 29 April 1963

Working	Loco	Time due off shed
Day shift	51	washing out
Herrington	52	12 midnight
Runner	57	5.00am
Washed duff runner	3	5.30am
D Pit washery	6	5.30am
Stone traffic (Nicholsons)	63	5.30am
D Pit pilot	33	5.30am
MAIN LINE	10	6.00am
Runner	30	6.00am
MAIN LINE	29	7.00am
Lumley Sixth Pit pilot	4	7.00am
Houghton Colliery pilot	2	7.30am
Coke Works pilot	53	8.00am
Philadelphia pilot	11	8.00am
Yard shunter	28	8.00am
Herrington (2ⁿᵈ shift)	52	8.00am

(Courtesy Colin E.Mountford)

Reorganisation of loco shifts as from 27 May 1968
(all 8¼-hour shifts)

Loco	Duty	Shift
59	Herrington	12 m'nt - 8.15am
42	Runners	5.00am - 1.15pm
58	Runners	5.30am - 1.45pm
2	Lambton 'D' washery	5.30am - 1.45pm
51	Coke Works	6.30am - 2.45pm
63	Central Landsale Depot	7.00am - 3.15pm
7	Runners	8.00am - 4.15pm
45	Philadelphia pilot/spare	8.00am - 4.15pm
59	Runners	9.00am - 5.15pm
2	Lambton 'D' washery	1.30pm - 9.45pm
42	Runners	1.30pm - 9.45pm
58	Runners	3.00pm-11.15pm

(Courtesy Colin E.Mountford)

Loco shifts:

15 February 1969 (last day of steam working)

Job	Loco
'D' washer	7
Runner (Houghton)	29
Runner (New Pit)	5
Coke Works	59
Central Depot	diesel (12120)

17 February 1969 (first day of 'all diesel' working)

Loco	Shift
12120	4.00am - 12.15pm
D9504	5.30am - 1.45pm
D9540	5.30am - 1.45pm
12119	6.00am - 2.15pm
(D9525)	7.00am - 3.15pm

(Courtesy Colin E.Mountford)

In the glory days, when working over BR metals from Penshaw sidings to Pallion Junction, over the branch and on to the staiths, the 0-6-2Ts were capable of working thirty loaded 16-ton wagons over the line. But those days were over and traffic on the railway was now much reduced. This was reflected by the number of stored locomotives in the old four road shed at Philadelphia – it contained five of the big 0-6-2Ts (Nos.10, 30, 31, 42 and 52) and various 0-6-0 and 0-4-0 saddle tanks. They were all intact but were cold and lifeless, standing forlornly in the roofless shed. It was a remarkable sight, but one that did not bode well for the future.

I returned to Philadelphia for what proved to be my last visit on 25 January 1969. By this time diesels had arrived. There were five diesels to be seen, and all had been purchased from British Railways. Three were Swindon-built 'Class 14' 0-6-0 diesel-hydraulics, ex-BR D9504, D9525 and D9540, and two were Derby-built shunters Nos.12119 and 12120. At this time British Railways had been selling surplus diesel locomotives; basically, they had decided that they had no suitable work for the Class 14s and had far too many English Electric shunters for their requirements. It was almost a repeat of the situation nearly forty years previously!

The diesels were sharing the work with the remaining steamers. It was all rather depressing. Modernisation was arriving and it marked the end of nearly 120 years of steam

traction. To make matters worse, the out-of-use engines were being brought out of the large shed for the attentions of the oxyacetylene cutter.

The end of steam working on the old Lambton system came on 15 February 1969. From then on it was all diesel. During the last week of steam up to six locomotives were in use; these included the last two working 0-6-2Ts, Nos.5 and 29, which, happily, were both saved for preservation.

The Lambton system's three Austerities (surely the NCB's equivalent to the 'Black Fives'!) survived the cessation of steam working in the winter of 1968/9, all three being transferred to Derwenthaugh on the south bank of the River Tyne. Derwenthaugh shed supplied locomotives to work Clockburn Drift Mine and Derwenthaugh Coking Plant, the Austerities replacing some interesting old stock. They managed to survive working alongside a growing number of diesel units until 1972, when steam working was eliminated *(see Railway Bylines 4:12)*.

At the time of the cessation of steam working on the Lambton system, the old single-road shed attached to the engine

No.26 was the last 0-6-0 tender engine to remain on the Lambton system but, although it was not officially withdrawn until August 1962 (it was scrapped four months later), it had been out of use for a considerable time beforehand. This was one of the locomotives which had been built at the Lambton Engine Works. Here, though, the engine is most definitely not in its original guise. In the 1950s 0-6-0s Nos.9 and 26 were rebuilt at the Lambton Engine Works with new tender tanks; these featured a high, inset coal bunker which gave improved vision when running tender-first. While No.26 was being dealt with it was also given the 'V'-front cab which is seen here.

Hawthorn Leslie 0-4-0ST No.28 came new to the Lambton system in 1902 and remained on home territory for its entire life. This picture was taken at Philadelphia on 17 August 1965. PHOTOGRAPH: ERIC ASHTON COLLECTION

works at Philadelphia played host to J27 0-6-0 No.65894 which had been saved for preservation by the North Eastern Locomotive Preservation Group. This small shed was used for engines which were being tested after repair in the works, and also for boiler washouts. Another preserved BR locomotive to find refuge at Philadelphia from 1968 – albeit locked up and out of sight on my visits – was No.60007, SIR NIGEL GRESLEY. This was at a time when BR's ban on steam traction was in force, so Philadelphia provided very convenient accommodation for the A4 until the relaxation of BR's ban in 1972.

On the Lambton system, by all accounts the diesels performed adequately, if not spectacularly. However, they did not have too long in which to assert themselves as, after the long lay-off during the miners' strike of 1984, things were never the same again. Rail traffic from Herrington Colliery ceased on 5 March 1984 (the colliery closed in November 1985), which meant that the only work available for Philadelphia locomotives was on hire to National Smokeless Fuels for shunting at Lambton Coking Works and working the traffic to/ from BR at Penshaw. In July 1985 NSF switched to hiring a Class 08 diesel from BR and so, on 19 July, NCB workings over the former Lambton Railway came to an end. With the cessation of NCB working, Philadelphia sheds were closed.

However, the Lambton Engine Works remained open for a while for the repair of coal-cutting machinery and diesel locomotives from other collieries in the Durham area. A 400-yard stretch of double track was left in place to test the repaired locomotives, but the rest of the railway was lifted. Locomotive repairs continued at the engine works only until May 1987, and the works closed completely on 22 December 1989. As for

the former Lambton Railway, the last section, between Lambton Coking Works and Penshaw, had been taken out of use in April 1986.

In December 1993 the last colliery in County Durham – Wearmouth Colliery, near Monkwearmouth – closed. It was the end of an era and, for many, a way of life. Fortunately, though, the whole of the Lambton Engine Works buildings – including the fitting shop and its famous clock – were granted the status of listed buildings and remain in engineering use, albeit non-railway, to this day. One of the old Philadelphia engine sheds also survives, and the 'railway area' around the shed buildings is now open grass.

Preservation
Fortunately, four of the former Lambton steam locomotives were saved for preservation. They are:
0-6-2T No.5: acquired by the North Eastern Locomotive Preservation Group in July 1970 and went to the North York Moors Railway; it is still there.
0-4-0ST No.14: left Philadelphia in 1962 (see table) but returned in October 1968; acquired by the North of England Open Air Museum in July 1970 but did not move to their store at Marley Hill until December 1972. It is now at Beamish.
0-6-2T No.29: acquired by the North Eastern Locomotive Preservation Group in June 1970 and went to the North York Moors Railway, Grosmont; it is still there.
0-6-2T No.52: went to the Keighley & Worth Valley Railway, Haworth. As TVR No.85 it is in full working order and is in very regular use.

Three diesels which had stints on the Lambton system were also saved for preservation:
No.506: sold to the Kent & East Sussex Railway in September 1987; it is still there.
No.513: sold by National Smokeless

Fuels to Mr.P.Miller in September 1985 and moved to the North Tyneside Steam Railway in January 1987. At the time of writing it is with the South Yorkshire Railway Preservation Society at Wincobanks.
No.101: sold to the Bowes Railway in August 1979; it is still there.

Author's note: *During the preparation of this article, various Industrial Railway Society handbooks and publications (particularly the* Industrial Railway Record No.151) *were consulted. Thanks are also due to Messrs. Colin Mountford and Roger Hateley for their invaluable advice, assistance and contributions to this article.*

Top left. *No.27 is reputed to have been built in 1845 as a 2-4-0 for the Newcastle & Darlington Junction Railway and rebuilt as an 0-6-0 in 1864. It was later rebuilt as a saddle tank, and was sold in this form to the Lambton company in 1898. It was rebuilt with side tanks at the Lambton Engine Works in 1904. This much-altered machine survived until December 1968 but, by this time, very little, if anything, of the original could have remained. This picture was taken at Philadelphia on 17 August 1965. PHOTOGRAPH: ERIC ASHTON COLLECTION*

Bottom left. *On of the Lambton Engine Works's more remarkable creations was 0-6-0PT No.6 which was built there in 1957/58. It incorporated parts from Coulthard 0-6-0s Nos.7 and 8 and Hawthorn 0-6-0ST No.39. It was scrapped in October 1964. This picture was taken at Philadelphia in June 1961. PHOTOGRAPH: PHIL LYNCH*

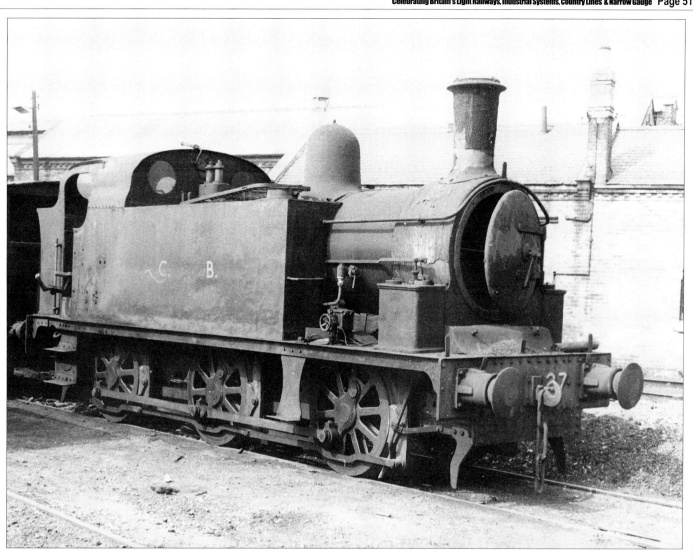

A little to the south of Philadelphia – the village can be seen in the mid-distance and the winding gear of Dorothea Colliery is on the right – Hawthorn Leslie 0-4-0ST No.47 is shunting what appears to be a stores van. The year is 1965. No.47 came to the Lambton system new in 1923 and remained until *circa* December 1968 when it was transferred to Hylton Colliery. It was scrapped at Hylton in June 1972. In the far distance on the left is Penshaw Monument. PHOTOGRAPH: V.WAKE; COURTESY THE ARMSTRONG TRUST

RSH 0-6-0ST No.8 belches smoke across the village while crossing the road at Philadelphia on 24 February 1968. PHOTOGRAPH: BRIAN SYDDALL

Although our article is principally about Philadelphia, a fascinating aspect of 'Philly' operations was that the NCB locomotives based there worked on BR metals to Sunderland. There weren't too many other places in the land where industrial locomotives had such lengthy runs on BR tracks. These 'industrials on BR' workings presented scope for photographs that were a little bit different (especially if Ian Carr was behind the camera), so we are pleased to include a selection of 'out on the road' pictures. This is Robert Stephenson 0-6-2T No.10 trundling through Sunderland. It is approaching Fawcett Street Junction Signal Box with a load of coal for South Dock on 20 August 1965. After this section of line closed it was turned into a walkway, but is now in the process of being turned back into a railway as part of the Tyne & Wear Metro extension. PHOTOGRAPH: IAN S.CARR

Kitson 0-6-2T No.31, with its distinctive, if not pretty, slanted cab, crosses the A1052 at Fencehouses with a train of empties from the exchange sidings for Lambton Coke Works. The BR signal box on the left controlled both BR and NCB lines over the crossing. The photographer is standing on the footbridge of Fencehouses station. PHOTOGRAPH: V.WAKE; COURTESY THE ARMSTRONG TRUST

Robert Stephenson 0-6-2T No.42 and a train of loaded coal wagons at Penshaw North, 26 August 1964. The train had originated at Harraton Colliery and had travelled on BR metals via Washington (where it had reversed) and Victoria Bridge. Another reversal will be required at Penshaw Yard before the ensemble can set out – this time with the engine running smokebox-first – to Sunderland. The bridge abutments on the NCB lines to the right of the signal box used to carry a wagonway to the River Wear. Penshaw North signal box is up on the gantry – this position gave the signalmen a better view of all the lines in the vicinity. Gantry 'boxes were a fairly common feature on the old NER – more so than on any other company. PHOTOGRAPH: IAN S.CARR

Penshaw – take two... Now-preserved Kitson 0-6-2T No.29 awaits the road to the BR line with a train for Sunderland Staiths. The date is 26 August 1957. The distinctive signal box can be seen in the distance just beyond the old wagonway embankment. The bridge abutments on the right are – or were – another part of the wagonway. This angle gives a reasonable view of No.29's rounded cab roof. This was a feature of many Lambton engines as, if they were employed on 'main line' runs or duties at the staiths on the River Wear, they had to be able to negotiate the tight bore of the tunnel from the Deptford branch to the staiths. PHOTOGRAPH: IAN S.CARR

The engines employed at Lambton Staiths on the River Wear had their own two-road shed at the landward end of the staiths complex. In the 1950s it was usual to find eight engines based there. On 26 April 1964 'Austerity' No.39 was taking water outside the shed while Hawthorn Leslie 0-4-0ST No.35 looked after some shunting. In the distance, the single-track tunnel on the right leads to Hetton Staiths (the tunnel was built after the Lambton and Hetton companies merged in 1911) while the double-track tunnel to its left is on the running line from the Deptford branch. The limited clearances of the tunnels are evident – it was this factor which necessitated the use of locomotives with 'cut down' cab roofs. PHOTOGRAPH: IAN S.CARR

On 25 January 1969 – just a couple of weeks of so before the end of steam working at Philadelphia – one of the NCB's ex-BR 'Class 14' diesel-hydraulics draws a couple of the disused steamers out of the sheds for scrapping. A number of 'Class 14s' were purchased by the NCB for use in the north-east, but most finished up at Ashington. Their replacements at Philadelphia were ex-BR 0-6-0 diesel-mechanicals. The concentration of a certain locomotive type at a certain location was a sensible bit of standardisation. PHOTOGRAPH: BRIAN SYDDALL

THE GWR'S WELSH INHERITANCE

As a result of the grouping the GWR inherited a good few hundred locomotives which were most decidedly 'non-Swindon'. One was GWR No.190, a Barclay 0-6-2T which had been built for the Alexandra Docks & Railway in 1908. Although the GWR fitted it with a shorter tank (the original one extended to the front of the smokebox) and standard safety valve cover, it otherwise remained substantially unaltered. It survived until April 1948 – this had been a fair innings for an absorbed engine which had eluded extensive 'Swindonisation'. It had spent its entire life – ADR, GWR and BR – allocated to Newport Pill shed. That is where this picture was taken in August 1934. PHOTOGRAPH: W.G.BOYDEN; COURTESY FRANK HORNBY

GWR No.1316 had been built for the Barry Railway in 1898. It was one of the Barry's eleven-strong 'J' class passenger tanks, three of which were built by Hudswell Clarke and the others (including the one seen here) by Sharp Stewart. Although five of the class were 'Swindonised' in the mid-1920s, No.1316 remained largely in its original condition. It was withdrawn in October 1928. The modified engines fared little better; indeed, the class was extinct by July 1930. This picture was taken at Barry (1316's lifetime home) in May 1927. PHOTOGRAPH: W.G.BOYDEN; COURTESY FRANK HORNBY

Several of the South Wales companies favoured 0-6-2Ts and, after the Grouping, the idea was taken on board by the GWR, the result being the GWR's own 56XX class engines. This, however, did not bring about the immediate demise of all the absorbed 0-6-2Ts; many were rebuilt with standard GWR features and went on to give excellent service until well into the 1950s. One such was GWR No.69, a former Rhymney Railway 'A1' class engine which had been built by Robert Stephenson & Co in 1918. Its archetypal 'Swindon' features – taper boiler, safety valve cover etc etc – are evident. No.69 survived until July 1955, having latterly lived at Duffryn Yard shed at Port Talbot. That is where this picture was taken on 7 June 1953. PHOTOGRAPH: FRANK HORNBY

For our final picture we return to decidedly 'non-Swindon' fare. This is GWR No.1383, a former Barry Railway 'H' class 0-8-2T which had been built in 1896 for working heavy coal trains. Only two of the seven 'Hs' were modified by the GWR – No.1383 was one of the two, being fitted with a GWR smokebox, chimney and safety valves and a new bunker. These hefty engines were soon deemed superfluous, the GWR's own 56XXs and 42XXs being considered adequate for the coal traffic, and all seven 'Hs' were withdrawn by 1930. This picture was taken at Barry shed on 1 May 1927. In this and the other three pictures, note the small 'G W R' letters above the engine's number – this was a feature of all GWR locomotives which had not been built or designed by the company. PHOTOGRAPH: W.G.BOYDEN; COURTESY FRANK HORNBY

LAST TRAIN TO ALVA

Words and pictures by W.A.C.Smith

J36 No.65307 at Alva with the 3.48pm to Alloa on 5 October 1953.

The 3½-mile long Alva branch in Clackmannanshire extended from Cambus Junction, on the Stirling-Dunfermline line, into an area known as the Hillforts. The branch was opened in June 1863 by a small local company but was soon acquired by the Edinburgh & Glasgow Railway which, in July 1865, became part of the North British Railway. So, in only a little over two years the Alva branch had had three owners. The branch lost its passenger services on 1 November 1954, and on 24 February 1964 it was cut back at the only intermediate station at Menstrie & Glenochil (two miles from Cambus Junction) to serve the Glenochil Yeast factory. The Cambus Junction-Menstrie section was later worked as a siding. It remained in use until 1994.

My first visit to the branch was on Monday 5 October 1953. I arrived at Alloa by the 2.28pm train from Stirling to Dollar, hauled by Pickersgill 4-4-0 No.54467, and spent the princely sum of one shilling for my ticket for the trip to Alva and back. I duly joined the 2.55pm for Alva which consisted of J36 No.65307 (62C) running tender-first with two non-corridor coaches. It was sparsely filled. The train departed on time and set out on the two-mile run to Cambus station; after getting the single-line tablet at the Junction 'box, we took to the branch, crossed the River Devon and curved under the Tullibody road into Menstrie & Glenochil station which had a siding into the yeast factory (a former distillery). Beyond the station and siding was a level crossing. A straight stretch, flanked by the

---

B.R. 14300/56

BRITISH TRANSPORT COMMISSION

T. H. HOLLINGSWORTH
Commercial Superintendent

C. J. H. SELFE
Asst. Commercial Superintendent

Telephone
DOUGLAS 7900
Ext. 294.

Telegraphic Address
COMMERCIAL CENTRAL
GLASGOW

BRITISH RAILWAYS

COMMERCIAL
SUPERINTENDENT
SCOTTISH REGION
CENTRAL STATION
GLASGOW, C.1

Our Reference
N.5878.
Your Reference

29th. October, 1954.

W.A.C. Smith Esqr.,
46 St. Andrew's Drive,
Glasgow, S.1.

Dear Sir,

I am obliged for your letter of the 26th. October and have made arrangements for the 1.3 p.m. Alloa to Alva to leave at 1.08 p.m. on Saturday, 30th. October. This will mean that the 1.28 p.m. Alva to Alloa will also require to be retimed to run 5 minutes later.

The day return tickets will be available for the passengers travelling on the 12.12 p.m. train from Glasgow (Buchanan Street).

Yours faithfully,

for T. H. HOLLINGSWORTH

The last day of scheduled passenger services on the Alva branch was Saturday 30 October 1954. Here, No.67466 waits at Alva with the very last train, the 1.33pm to Alloa.

The last down train on the Alva branch was the retimed 1.08pm from Alloa. The stop at Menstrie & Glenochil provided the opportunity for photographs. It seems a tad ironic that the station was treated to the 'new timetable' notice only six weeks or so before it was itself erased from the passenger railway map.

Table 78								Ex Sats		Ex Sats		Ex Sats	
Miles	**WEEKDAYS ONLY**	a.m.			a.m.			p.m		p.m		p.m	
98	Edinburgh (Wav.) ... lev.	6 8	..	..	1040*	..	..	1 25	..	..	..	4 25	..
77	Glasgow (Queen St.) lev.	..	..	..	*1180E	..	..	1B35	..	..	..	4 57	..
..	Alloa ... ... lev.	7 28	..	..	1 p 3	..	..	2 55	..	4 30	..	6 0	..
2	Cambus (for Tullibody) ...	7 33	..	..	1 8	..	..	3 1	..	4 35	..	6 5	..
4	Menstrie and Glenochil ...	7 39	..	..	1 13	..	..	3 6	..	4 40	..	6 10	..
5½	Alva ... ... arr.	7 42	..	..	1 17	..	..	3 10	..	4 44	..	6 14	..

Table 78						Sats only		Ex Sats		Ex Sats		Ex Sats		Ex Sats			
	WEEKDAYS ONLY	a.m.		a.m.			p.m		p.m		p.m		p.m		p.m			
	Alva ... ... lev.	6 55	..	8 40	..	..	1 28	..	2 2	..	3 48	..	5 0	..	6 22	..	..	..
	Menstrie and Glenochil ...	7 6	..	8 45	..	..	1 32	..	2 6	..	3 52	..	5 5	..	6 26	..	..	..
	Cambus (for Tullibody) ...	7 11	..	8 50	..	..	1 37	..	2 11	..	3 58	..	5 10	..	6 32	..	..	..
	Alloa ... ... arr.	7 15	..	8 54	..	..	1 41	..	2 15	..	4 2	..	5 14	..	6 36	..	..	..
77	Glasgow (Queen St.) arr.	3K50	..	1018K	..	..	3K15	..	4K22	..	5K27	..	6 55	..	9K12	..	..	..
98	Edinburgh (Wav.) ... arr.	9 42	..	1135E	..	..	3 19	..		..	5 43	..	7 36	..	9 30	..	..	..

Scottish Region public timetable, 14 June to 19 September 1954.

Above. **A fascinating view of the very seldom photographed station at Alva on the 'last day', 30 October 1954.**

Ochil Hills, brought us to the small terminus at Alva one minute late at 3.11pm.

I took a photograph at Alva and waited for the return trip which was due to depart at 3.48pm. As I was the only passenger for the return trip the elderly Alloa driver, by the name of Robertson, and his mate Doyle invited me to travel on the footplate. They provided me with gloves "to keep your hands clean". They remarked that No.65307 was better than the usual 'Tankie' (a C15 4-4-2T); they added that the Glens (D34 4-4-0s) were 'good engines', but dismissed the Caley Bogies (4-4-0s) as 'riding like tramcars'. Coincidentally, I was to return to Glasgow via Alloa Bridge (on the 4.25pm from Perth to Queen Street) behind one of these 'tramcars'!

Just over a year later, on 26 October 1954, selected newspapers carried the formal notice of withdrawal of the passenger services to Alva as from Monday 1 November. This had been approved by the Scottish Transport Users Consultative Committee, partly on the grounds that 'frequent bus services operate in the area'. In the absence of Sunday services on the Alva branch, the last public trains were therefore on Saturday 30th October. However, as will be seen from the accompanying timetable, on Saturdays there were no trains in the afternoon – the very last return working of that day was 1.03pm from Alloa, returning at 1.28pm from Alva. As my employment in Glasgow at that time (pre-BR) required my presence on a Saturday morning, this seemed to rule out attendance at the last rites until closer examination of the timetables revealed that, on Saturdays, a 12.51pm from Larbert (which connected with the 12.12pm Oban train from Buchanan Street) arrived at Alloa a mere two minutes after the scheduled departure of the Alva train. With youthful optimism I wrote off to Scottish Region Commercial Superintendent at Central station requesting that the Alva train await the arrival of the train from Larbert (in retrospect one might ask why this had not been done on a regular basis) and I received a commendably prompt reply explaining that this had been arranged – the departure of the Alva train was retimed for five minutes later.

Come Saturday, at midday I was to be found at Buchanan Street purchasing a day return to Alva. It cost me 4/8d. Given that this day was a rather significant one for the Alva branch, I was a little disappointed that the booking clerk did not query my request. As planned, I caught the 12.12pm Oban train from Buchanan Street; it was hauled by Black Five No.45115. It delivered me to Larbert punctually at 12.44pm and, after a wait of about five minutes, Caley 0-4-4T No.55214 arrived with the 12.35pm ex-Grangemouth. It left on time at 12.51pm, crossing waterlogged countryside (the weather had been so bad in Scotland that the Caley and GSW main lines had been closed due to flooding) and over the River Forth. There was an agonising near stop for signals before we could join the Stirling line at Longcarse Junction, but we arrived at Alloa station at 1.06pm, only one minute late. I was met by the station foreman and conducted to the adjoining bay where C15 No.67466 stood bunker-first at the head of two non-corridors, SC82050E and SC80335E. It has to be said that my appearance was something of a disappointment to the thirty or so Alva-bound passengers who had been told that their train was awaiting a V.I.P!

The Alva train departed at the revised time of 1.08pm. It exploded a succession of detonators. Most of the 'ordinary' passengers left the train at Cambus, leaving just a handful of regulars – who were outnumbered by us enthusiasts – to continue to Menstrie and Alva. Beyond Menstrie we had a good view of the work which was in progress on sinking a new colliery (Glenochil Colliery); the colliery was provided with a rail connection, but was to remain in production for only six years. Our arrival at Alva was greeted by more detonators and, as the engine rounded, I purchased an LNER single ticket to Menstrie as a souvenir. The ticket, which the clerkess obligingly clipped, was inscribed 5½d, but I was charged the then-current rate of only 4d – surely a rare example of a reduction in fare.

After the obligatory photographs had been taken at Alva – the train having specially positioned for this purpose – our departure at the booked time of 1.33pm was watched by quite a few locals. On the return trip a stop was made at Menstrie to pick up the crossing keeper and, although the station was already locked up, there were more detonators as we pulled out for the last time. Two enthusiasts left the train at Cambus, but the rest of us continued to Alloa where we arrived two minutes late at 1.48pm. The engine then went to the small shed (sub to Dunfermline) to join J35s Nos.64475 and 64493, J36 No.65307 and J88 No.68351. The J36 had worked the morning service on the Alva branch and had 'The Last Round Up' chalked on its smokebox door.

I left Alloa on the 2.45pm Stirling-Perth, travelling over the Devon Valley line. We were hauled by D34 No.62470 GLEN ROY. I returned from Perth to Glasgow by way of the main line, my train being hauled by Jubilee No.45673 KEPPEL.

This, however, was not my last visit to Alva for, as the accompanying photographs show, it was included in the itineraries of railtours in 1962 and 1963. There was a later railtour as well – this was the 'Scottish Rambler No.5' of Easter 1966 which was propelled from Cambus to Menstrie by J38 No.65914. By this time the station at Menstrie had been bulldozed away and the line between there and Alva had been lifted.

The joint RCTS/SLS Scottish railtour of 1962 lasted from the 14th to the 23rd of June. There were no less than 153 participants for the first three days and 123 for the remainder of the days. On Monday 18 June the tour train started at Perth and took in Dunblane (where No.256 GLEN DOUGLAS took over), Killin Junction, Killin and Loch Tay, before heading south to Stirling. After the engine had turned at Stirling the train continued to Cambus where J36 No.65345 was waiting to work the five-coach set on to Alva. This picture was taken at Alva – note how herbaceous the station has become since the cessation of ordinary passenger services in 1954.

Right. The tour train of 18 June 1962 passes Menstrie on its return trip from Alva to Alloa. The train returned to Alloa; the tour train engine, GLEN DOUGLAS, was waiting there, having run ahead from Cambus to Alloa. From Alloa the tour train continued via the Devon Valley line to Perth. *(Editor's note: The rail tour was considered a huge success on all fronts. A report of the whole tour appeared in the October 1962 edition of the* Railway Observer *and included the note: 'Especial thanks are also due to Mr.W.A.C.Smith who was responsible for an excellent itinerary...'. At the risk of causing our contributor to blush, that Mr.Smith is the very same Mr.Smith as the one who provided this feature).*

Bottom right. Cambus station, looking west, on 15 April 1967. It closed with the withdrawal of the Stirling-Dunfermline service on 7 October 1968. The old Alva branch can be seen heading off to the right beyond the footbridge though, by the time this picture was taken, the branch had been truncated at Menstrie.

Below. The 'Scottish Rambler No.2' railtour of 1963 was jointly organised by the Scottish Area of the SLS and the Branch Line Society. On 13 April it visited the Alva branch – this is the tour train, headed by J36 No.65323, between Alva and Menstrie.

RUMMAGING FOR RELICS - On the trail of the Lee Moor Tramway

Many railway enthusiasts, particularly those of 'a certain age' (i.e. old enough to remember when Britain still had a nearly full set of branch lines and minor railways), enjoy a nostalgic rummage on old trackbeds. A search for relics of a favourite long lost line or station or whatever can be very addictive. In the case of MAURICE DART, one of his favourite 'long lost' lines is the Lee Moor Tramway, the 4ft 6in gauge line which extended from Laira Wharf at Plymouth to the china clay workings at Lee Moor, on the south-west edge of Dartmoor. Although the Plymouth end of the tramway remained in use until 1960, most of the rest of the line had fallen into disuse well before then. This feature reveals some of the fruits of Maurice Dart's explorations along the upper parts of the route in later years.

1. The original Torycombe Incline rose 300 feet in 649 yards to take the tramway from the china clay works at Lee Moor up towards the workings. At Grid Ref SX569613 (approx.) the incline passed between the stone walls – which I had always assumed to be bridge abutments – seen here, but there was a long-standing mystery about what used to pass *over* the bridge. Fortunately, though, a colleague who was born at Lee Moor and is well versed in the history and development of the area was able to unravel the mystery for me. Apparently, in the early 1800s Torycombe was connected to Lee Moor village by a rough track which climbed the hillside. About a quarter of the way up the hill at a spot called Broad Oaks there was a small quarry on the north side of the rough track, and unwanted spoil from this was dumped on the

opposite side of the track. During 1853 work commenced on the construction of the Lee Moor Tramway which included an incline from the area of the brick works at Torycombe to the east of the level crossing up to Black Alder Tor (to the west of Lee Moor village); this incline crossed the rough track at Broad Oaks and therefore had to pass through the spoil from the adjacent quarry. To achieve this a cutting was created – the spoil was piled up on each side of the tramway and stout walls, built of stone from the quarry, were constructed on either side so as to prevent slippage. So, going back to my original query about what crossed the bridge over the incline, the answer was 'nothing', as it wasn't a bridge after all. This picture was taken on 15 April 1993.

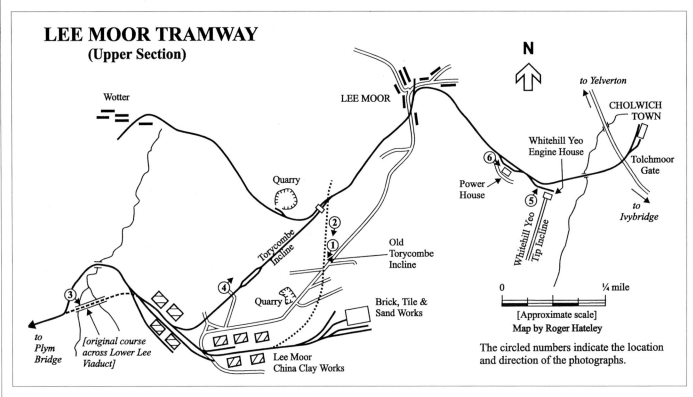

LEE MOOR TRAMWAY
(Upper Section)

Wotter

LEE MOOR

N

to Yelverton

CHOLWICH TOWN

Quarry

Whitehill Yeo Engine House

Tolchmoor Gate

Torycombe Incline

Power House

to Ivybridge

Old Torycombe Incline

Whitehill Yeo Tip Incline

Quarry

Brick, Tile & Sand Works

0   ¼ mile

[Approximate scale]
Map by Roger Hateley

to Plym Bridge

[original course across Lower Lee Viaduct]

Lee Moor China Clay Works

The circled numbers indicate the location and direction of the photographs.

2. Having looked at the 'bridge abutments', I turned, crossed the road, and walked up the next part of the incline. This picture looks down towards the previous vantage point, the cutting between the 'abutments' being visible a little to the right of the bus shelter. The building in the valley way below is on the site of the old Lee Moor sand plant. The path on which I was standing to take this picture is identifiable as an old tramway incline, but let's not forget that this was the 'first' Torycombe Incline – it was in use for only about six months during 1856 and was soon replaced by a completely new incline about a quarter-mile to the west.

3. If you thought that the Lee Moor tramway is a bit of a 'long lost' line, then Lower Lee Viaduct has been lost for much, much longer. When built in 1854 the tramway originally crossed the valley of the Wotter Brook just to the west of Torycombe by means of a viaduct. The viaduct was 205 yards long and approximately 70 feet high; the original intention had been that it should have seventeen wooden piers, but it was constructed with only fifteen. It was said to be unsteady in rough weather. In 1878 a new section of tramway was opened through Lee Woods on what was known as the Wotter Curve (this followed the natural contours of the land) and the original section across the viaduct was abandoned. It was dismantled during 1880, but 113 years later – on 15 April 1993 – the western abutment (approximate grid reference SX560611) was still perched somewhat precariously on the steeply sloping hillside above Portworthy Mica Dam. The abutment was, however, the only visible remains of the old viaduct by this time, though the old trackbed was still discernible to the right of the abutment. Part of one of the piers remains buried in the mica dam.

Above. 4. Now, what did we say about exploring old trackbeds? If that is one of your pastimes, then you will be very, very familiar with views such as this. Well – views something like this... This is, in fact, the upper section of the 1 in 7 Torycombe Incline (the 'new' incline of 1858) which closed in 1939. Its alignment subsequently became popular as a footpath between the china clay works and the outskirts of Lee Moor village. This picture was taken in August 1955.

Top right. 5. The tramway originally continued from Lee Moor China Clay Works, up Torycombe Incline, past Lee Moor village, and terminated on the north-east side of the Yelverton-Ivybridge road near the hamlet of Cholwich Town. About ¼-mile or so before the end of the line was the tip incline winding house at Whitehill Yeo (pronounced locally as either 'Whydleyeo' or, by real old timers, as 'Whydeeyeo'). In this picture, passing from left to right behind the winding house, marked by a series of fence posts, is the trackbed of the upper section of the Lee Moor Tramway – to the left is Lee Moor village and then Torycombe incline, while to the right is Tolchmoor Gate and Cholwich Town. This section of the tramway had fallen into disuse by 1933. The engine house was served by a siding from the tramway – the siding was used for coal deliveries. The incline, which was used to haul wagons of sand up from the micas, was in use from 1900 until 1925; it was about 300 yards long and had gradients of 1 in 3, 1 in 11 and 1 in 15. The winding house itself was at grid reference SX578617. To take this photograph in August 1955 I had to scramble up the tip incline from which some 30,000 tons of sand had been washed away during a violent rainstorm the previous year. It wasn't easy! But at least I was able to obtain a pictorial record of the building as it has now disappeared, much of the area having been used for the expansion of the china clay works.

Bottom right. 6. A few yards to the north-west of Whitehill Yeo winding house was Lee Moor Old Power Station (the chimney of the latter is on the left of this picture). It was served by a siding which dropped steeply at 1 in 30 from the tramway – in this picture the trackbed of the tramway itself is on the far left, and in the gully immediately to its right is the bed of the old siding. The siding was used to bring in supplies of coal and oil. The building is still extant, but is no longer used for its original purpose. This picture was taken in August 1955.

RIGHT AWAY, WEST RIDING

by Richard Hardy

RICHARD HARDY's railway career started with the LNER at Doncaster in January 1941. His work soon took him to the West Riding and, during his four-year stint there, he developed, not only a great fondness for that area and its railways, but also a great respect for the local enginemen. Indeed, his West Riding days shaped his life for a lengthy and successful career on the railways.

This is a story of some of the railways of the West Riding of Yorkshire in the war years between 1941 and 1945. Although I worked on engines for many, many miles in the West Riding, as a Doncaster apprentice I was of the LNER Southern Area. Those 'Geordie' folk, as we knew them (whether they came from Newcastle, Hull or wherever!), had their own station in Leeds and used the LMS (Midland) station in Bradford to which I have never been in my life; the Midland shed at Manningham might have been on the moon for all I cared, whilst Low Moor, a few miles from Bradford Exchange which we shared with the LMS (L&Y), was a 'Lanky' shed, but I knew not where. My 'home patch' in Bradford was Hammerton Steet, and it was all very parochial. However, the L&Y had some very good little engines, nearly up to ours, and we did speak to the 'Lanky' men when

we had the chance. But this tale is about the GN West Riding, an amazing railway with its ferocious gradients and its fire-throwing GN and GC engines which were often worked to their limit. It all started nearly sixty years ago and, as I have never taken notes nor engine numbers, you may well find an inaccuracy here and there. But my memory will never falter when I write of those many enginemen at Copley Hill, Bradford and Ardsley who set out, for no other reason than kindness, to teach a seventeen-year old boy everything they could about their job and the engines they worked. They said: "One day you are going to be a boss and you will be neither use nor ornament to us or the railway if you don't know our job inside out". Much of my experience was gained in my spare time, at night or at weekends, and I treasure every minute that I spent on the footplate, soaking up the atmosphere,

listening to and learning from men years older than myself, for even the firemen in those days were over forty years of age. I worked with Doncaster men, Grantham men, Grimsby men, Mexborough men, and even New England, Neasden and King's Cross men – and, of course, the Sheffield 'Grinders'. What wonderful times I had with Joe Oglesby of the GC sheds at Neepsend and Darnall. But this is a GN West Riding story...

We always said the West Riding began when you got on the Leeds road at Marshgate Junction. Any Leeds man would tell you that and a GN man would maintain it was *his* railway but, in fact, the West Riding and Grimsby Joint started at that point whilst the other part of the Joint line from Stainforth on the Doncaster-Hull-Cleethorpes line came in at Adwick Junction, north of Carcroft. The WR&G continued to the Joint station of Wakefield Westgate where there was still a strong GC influence. Closed in 1924, there had been a GC shed up against the wall on the up side by Balne Lane sidings and the turntable was still there and in use during the war. Wakefield GC was largely a freight shed but it used to work the 'Barnsley Bus' via Nostell North Junction and on to the GC round the corner

Left. On a summer evening in 1948, C14 7441 (ex-6121), climbs the 1 in 100 past Potovens Lane Crossing, just over a mile north of Wakefield Westgate. The train, which is a semi-fast to Leeds, has just passed Wrenthorpe North box. At this time Ardsley still had nine of the twelve C14s. PHOTOGRAPH: PETER WARD

Below. The GN station, Dewsbury Central, was high up over part of the town. It had an island platform and short tunnels at both ends. The Bradford-London expresses stopped here and there was a sparse service to Leeds Central over 'The Alps' via Tingley and Beeston Junction and a better one to Bradford Exchange via Batley and Drighlington. In this picture the C14 and its train of four articulated GN coaches could be going either way, but it is more than likely to be going to Bradford for the heavy London job which left at 17.06 and was worked by Ardsley men. This job, with its steep gradients, fully extended a good C14 and its crew. The start was easy rising at 1 in 390 to Batley Carr but then steepened to 1 in 89 and 1 in 53 for the run up to Batley station. Even with four little coaches, a fireman had to keep his wits about him and full boiler pressure was needed to start at the stations going up 'Batley 'Oil' (Batley Hole). The engine seen here is 7444 – it was a very good engine and one on which I made several journeys. It was formerly numbered 6124; it received its new number in April 1946 and retained that number until May 1952 when it became BR No.67444, so that narrows down the date of the picture. Am I right in thinking that there is a lucky young lad on the footplate while nobody bar the driver and photographer is about? PHOTOGRAPH: W.A.CAMWELL; PETER WARD COLLECTION

at Wintersett Junction; it had one 'Pom-Pom Bogie' (LNER class D9), No.105, which worked a daily job to Cleethorpes via Adwick Junction. The driver of 105 was a Mr.John Duckmanton whom I had the honour of meeting at his home one Sunday morning; he was one of the very old school who retired in 1924, a year after I was born. His son Horace was a fireman and went from Wakefield to Mexborough, thence to Gorton and finally to King's Cross where he shared the only A1, 60156, in a link of A4s, with Driver McKinley. He retired in 1966 when I was Divisional Manager at King's Cross and we spent two happy hours together in my office on his last day. He retired after fifty years service without a blemish on his record. His old father would have been proud of him.

Wakefield Kirkgate

It all started at Wakefield Kirkgate which I had previously thought to be pure 'Lanky' territory but it had, in fact, been a Joint L&Y and GN station. It was 22.10 on a Saturday evening in May 1941 – it was still daylight for we had double summer time during the war. Why I was at Kirkgate, not Westgate, I cannot recall, but wherever I had been, I was dirty, tired and scruffy. The London Mail ran in to Kirkgate from Leeds Central headed by a GC B4 No.6100, a shining green 'Immingham' and the regular engine for the Mail as far as Doncaster. I looked into the cab of that old B4 at the head of 17 coaches and was immediately accosted by the extrovert Copley Hill fireman who asked me who and what I was. I told him I was a Doncaster apprentice and I was, at once, invited to travel on the footplate to Doncaster. I had no pass but that meant nothing to those kind men who made me so much at home that night. The driver was Bob Foster, a GC man from Wakefield, in the top link, and had the war not come he would have been the first GC man in the Pullman link at Copley Hill. The fireman was not Bob's regular

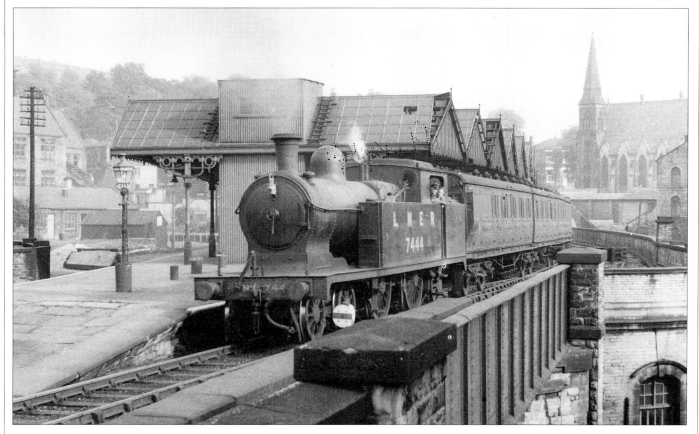

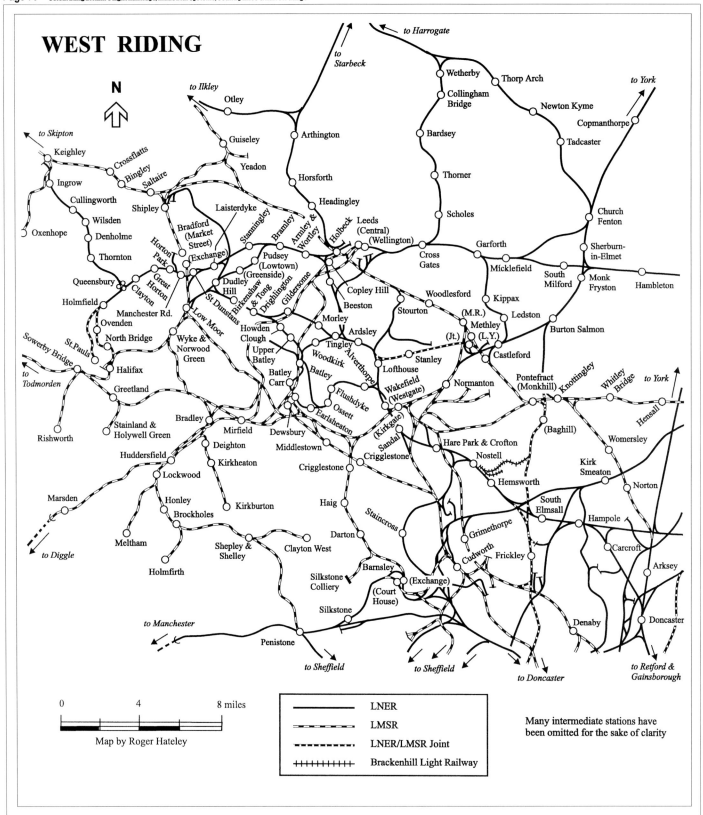

WEST RIDING

Map by Roger Hateley

LNER
LMSR
LNER/LMSR Joint
Brackenhill Light Railway

Many intermediate stations have
been omitted for the sake of clarity

mate Harry Bradshaw (who had asked
for the night off), but a 'Young Hand' with
nineteen years service. So it was Stan
Hodgson and Bob Foster who opened up
my life to the wonders of the West Riding.

We set off from Kirkgate without a slip
with our huge train, round the sharp curve
and along the L&Y to Crofton Junction
where we took the WR&G spur to the main
line at Hare Park and then away we went
to Doncaster up the 1 in 150 to Nostell. I
can remember the tremendous roar from
the chimney as Bob opened up 6100 on to
the big valve as we swung across the
junction just short of Hare Park station; I
also remember how freely the old engine
coasted from South Elmsall right up to

Marshgate distant. As we ran into
Doncaster I was told to get up in the corner
out of sight, and when we had unhooked
and turned on the angle and come to rest
in the Garden Sidings, my future
education began and continued into the
early hours. I was instructed how to take
water, to trim coal, how to look after
myself when up on the tender and, later,
how to hold and swing a shovel, how to
stand and how to build up a fire so that
the engine would remain quiet but with
the damper open, without smoke or
blowing off steam and yet have a great
fire ready to set off to Leeds once more
with 17, even 18 cars. When I eventually
left them, Bob said: "Come in a fortnight's

time and we'll see what we can do". Had I
been at Westgate instead of at Kirkgate
on that fateful night I might have met
Alistair Kerr, later Deputy County Land
Agent who was well known to many of the
Leeds, Bradford and Ardsley men for his
great interest in railway work. But that
was a pleasure not long deferred and he,
in turn, introduced me to Ted Hailstone
from whom, as you will read, I was to learn
so much.

My early journeys on 6100 were on the
Mail from Leeds Central when all was
quiet and the first stop would be less than
a mile away at Holbeck, a long island
platform above the low level station. We
would be loading for the best part of ten

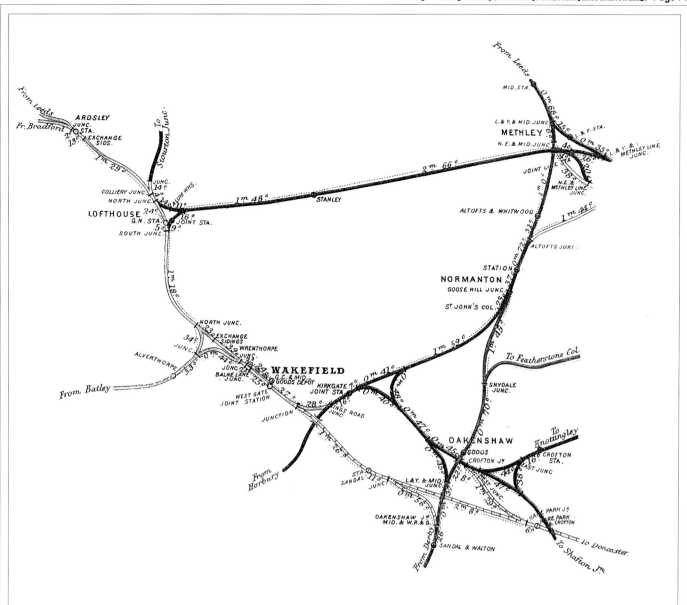

This and the other similar maps are Railway Clearing House plans. The originals were in colour, hence the occasional differences in tones. The different colours on the originals were to identify individual (pre-Grouping) railway companies; however, the maps are included here simply to show what lines went where, and we trust that the loss of colours does not detract.

minutes and then we would climb up by Copley Hill shed at 1 in 50, with that left trailing axlebox thumping hard underneath us, and at about 20mph with our heavy train we would pass Wortley South Junction and then away downhill to rush the 1 in 100 up to Ardsley and into the tunnel. On the way up, we would roar past Beeston Junction where the line to Batley over 'The Alps' diverged to go climbing up and up and up at 1 in 51 until it crossed us by a high viaduct before we dived into Ardsley Tunnel. We stopped at Ardsley as one of the Running Foremen lived there and sometimes rode up the bank to sample 6100 when he was late turn. Then we dropped down at 1 in 132/ 100, coasting past the junction for Castleford, through Lofthouse and its nearby colliery, past Wrenthorpe yards and down into Westgate where the Bradford portion would be attached in the rear, so we had to run right down well past the platform end.

Leeds-Castleford

Now, let us start from Leeds Central one Saturday afternoon in 1943. Alf Cartwright and I are going to Castleford

with an N1, 3190, and four old GN coaches. 3190 was the first of the breed and the only one with long tanks, for she was too heavy for the Widened Lines from Moorgate to Kings Cross. For many years she had been a Leeds engine. The Castleford road was easy and we did not have to work hard once we passed Ardsley. Driver Alf Cartwright had enough confidence in me to send his mate, Percy Hudson, in the train and, as Copley Hill still had good Yorkshire coal, the turn was a doddle. Alf was an old GC man from Staveley – tall, heavy and looked far older than he was. He enjoyed firing and often changed over with his very experienced mate; this was all part of the 'Cartwright Act', as was the celluloid collar he wore, washing it under the tap each day! He had an advanced, slow speaking, deadpan and very droll sense of humour.

We stopped at Holbeck and on the approach to Beeston, the next station, we coasted to a quick stop at the empty platform. However, while I was screwing on the handbrake to prevent us rolling backwards on the 1 in 100, I was approached by the Stationmaster, a fiery little man with a fierce moustache who

told me in no uncertain tones to get to hell out of it as we were not supposed to stop at Beeston. Somewhat taken aback, for I was only young and Stationmasters were pretty high up the ladder, I asked Alf to have a word with the gentleman before he exploded. My driver shambled across the cab and looked down from a seemingly great height. In a most disarming and friendly manner and with the glimmer of a smile Alf drawled: "Well, Mister, it's a long time since we saw you, so we thought we'd call and see how you were goin' on." After that we got to hell out of it and with our light train were soon right time again. I doubt if anything was said. Alf hadn't checked his 'staff book' (working timetable) and the guard may not have said 'miss Beeston'. We shall never know for it happened fifty-seven years ago.

At Lofthouse North Junction we branched left for the Methley Joint Line (GN, L&Y and NE) and dropped downhill to Stanley and on towards Methley at quite a lick. It was mostly pithead country and before long we had joined the NE from Altofts Junction and pulled up at Castleford. It was a doddle, only 14 miles from Leeds and very different from the

Under the roof of Bradford Exchange on the GN side of the station and attached to an old North Eastern coach stands GC N5 9261 (ex-5527). This is the very engine which I had on my first trip with Ted Hailstone to Halifax. The C12s had gone, the B1s had arrived, but Bradford still had five N5s which were considered to be good enough to share the local work with N1s, C14s and the last of the 'Imminghams', a class which had borne the heat and burden of the heavy express work as well as endless 'specialing' before the war. I fear I never noticed such things at the time, but the plate on the cabside is the original Beyer Peacock works plate dated October 1893. This confirmed that 9261 was one of the early examples of this 129-strong class. She lasted until 1957 so she did not owe the company anything after years of hard and economical work. PHOTOGRAPH: PETER WARD

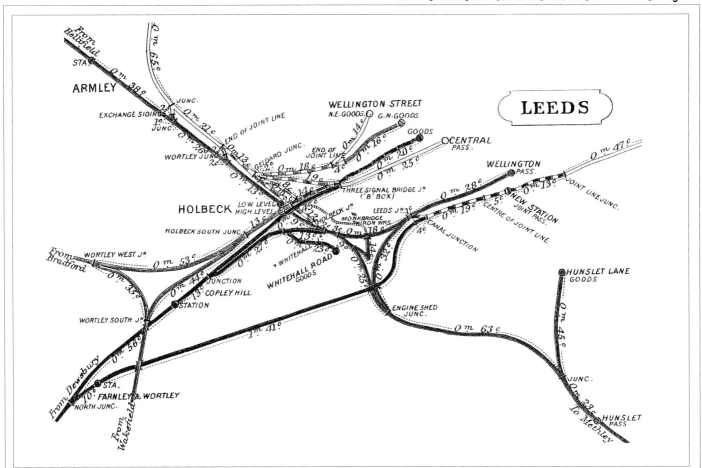

normal run of things in the West Riding. Just before we left the main line and near Lofthouse Colliery, we had passed the junction to the East and West Yorkshire Union Railway which was just over two miles long and connected the GN with the Midland at Stourton Junction. They had had their own engines at one time but the line was now worked largely by a 'Humpy', a GN J52; it was all freight work of course until after the war when the wife of the Rothwell stationmaster used to organise seaside excursions. The Loco Foreman of the E&W eventually became Shed Foreman at Copley Hill. His promotion had been slow of course, but 'Big Dick' Mitchinson was, I believe, a force to be reckoned with. I never met him, for in those days I kept as far from authority as possible. His son Jack was an apprentice at Doncaster, three years my senior; happily, we were to meet again many years later when I went to Liverpool.

Before we leave the Castleford road and tackle the really stern stuff, there was a lovely little job in No.1 Tanky link at Copley Hill that left Leeds Central at 17.23, all stations to Castleford and, in

the earlier '40s, was always hauled by one of the three C12s – 4010, 4014 and 4020 – those with the bogie brakes. They were good little engines dating back to 1898, simple, straightforward and strong for their size; they were usually sure-footed but they did tend to slip with a heavy train when getting away. They liked as short a cut-off as possible and full regulator, if necessary, whereupon they would bounce at the front end on their springs in time with each revolution, both amusing and attractive. Then they were very lively; the fireman could maintain the water level and they would steam freely, but only with a thin, white-hot fire and any number of rockets flying up the chimney.

But on the 17.23, there was no need for histrionics. At Castleford we pushed the train inside to let an LMS train go by and then dropped down to the platform once more. Actually, Castleford had been an NER station and we really were on foreign territory once we had left the main line and set off for Leeds City via Kippax, Garforth and Cross Gates, coming to rest a few minutes' walk from our starting point. After a suitable interval, we set off

quietly and anonymously in that alien world for all stations to Leeds Central. I had several trips with Bill Denman, a truly great engineman from whom I learned a great deal. Bill hailed from Retford (GC) and was very much at home on the GN Atlantics; his mate was the placid and easy-going Gilbert Gregory who did more firing than driving on the 'Tanky' jobs.

Wakefield-Bradford

Now for the Bradford expresses which were the rear four or five coaches of a down London express brought into Westgate by a Leeds K3 as though it would never stop, for Copley Hill men always ran at high speed over the ninety-nine arch viaduct with maybe a touch of the brake over the junction from Kirkgate. When I travel to Leeds today and we crawl portentously into Westgate, my mind goes back to the thrilling descent to Sandal on K3s, GN Atlantics and B4s whose drivers had such remarkable judgement of speed and brakepower.

My first journey on a Bradford express was with a J1 and five cars, a full load. These engines were a tender version of the wet steam N1s and had done amazing work before the war on excursion trains to the East Coast from the West Riding. We had 3005 and Bradford men, George Stoyles and George Barker. The former was a Brontë expert as well as a speed merchant and he gave 3005 a fearful larruping and, being an old-six wheeled engine, she felt every bump and corner of the road. George Barker had a tough time and he was well down for steam and water when we reached the top at Drighlington despite using the injector continuously. But I had never seen anything like it and,

Left. **Ex-Great Northern 4-4-2T 4020 was one of the original engines of 1898/99. One can see the bogie brakes which were fitted to those class members used in the West Riding. This is the 17.23 Leeds Central-Leeds City in the yard at Castleford in 1943. We have set back to let a Midland fast go by; soon we shall draw forward into the platform and away for Kippax, Garforth and Leeds City, deep in North Eastern territory. The engineman on the left is Alfie Hudson, a comical and very broad spoken ex-Bradford fireman who had been at Kings Lynn for a few years. The Norfolkers had had great difficulty with Alfie's dialect with its "thee and tha" and "coil and watter". He had been nicknamed 'Scufter' at Kings Lynn but became 'Twinkletoes' at Copley Hill. But wherever he went and whatever his nickname, he was a character. The guard is from Leeds Central and we had often had him on this job – he was always on the ball and friendly. On the right is Bill Denman, an ex-GC man from Retford, a truly great engineman and a man of charm and principle. He was at ease with all, quiet, gently smiling, a thinking man, indomitable in adversity and certainly one to get the best from Alfie.**
PHOTOGRAPH: RICHARD HARDY; THE TRANSPORT TREASURY

J50 8909 climbs the 1 in 55 between Earlsheaton and Osset. It is approaching Runtlings Junction. The train has probably come out of Dewsbury Goods and has shunted Earlsheaton. Six wagons and two brake vans will not test a good engine up 1 in 55 but twelve or fifteen loaded wagons would be a different matter. The J51s were known in the West Riding as 'Tango Tanks'; they were strong on the banks and had an excellent lookout for shunting with regulator and brake handles and reversing lever close at hand. During the war there were over twenty at Ardsley and another twenty at Bradford; Copley Hill had six and, of those, at least two had hopper bunkers which gave improved look-out when working bunker first and were used on the Leeds Central carriage pilot jobs.
PHOTOGRAPH: PETER WARD

my goodness, it whetted my appetite so that I came again and again.

The West Riding was a hard school. They said that if you could fire a small engine over those fearful gradients you could go anywhere. Perhaps that was stretching it a bit, but the point is that no engine would do its stuff unless the fireman, not only completely mastered the principles of combustion, but also met the demands of his engine and driver by firing in exactly the right places at the right time, as well as firing to the injector which would be set and then left alone with the steam remaining constant near the red mark. It sounds so easy but, in practice, it wasn't. Many a Bradford express stopped short of steam on the way up.

My last trip with an N1 was on VJ day, firing for Driver Harold Binder on the wet steamer N1, 4567. Harold was a lovely man and a great friend, but the trip was a disaster. Nothing went right. Instead of filling the boiler at Morley and staying for a few minutes, we chanced our arm, leaving on time. But we gradually faded so that we passed the summit with no more than 100psi. We started to go downhill and thought the day was won, but the water in the boiler was so low, out of sight in the bottom nut, that we had to start the second feed which knocked the pressure back to 80psi. On went the brake, and we stopped going downhill opposite Tong Cemetery, a very appropriate place. What a performance

and how Harold enjoyed it! It is an awful feeling when you see the vacuum needle falling and you know you can't do anything about it until you have had a blow up. On one occasion we stopped with 6131, a GC C14, a good engine though starting to blow off at 150psi which was a bit low. This time we didn't get as far as Tong and stuck fast across the crossing at Drighlington.

Those were the only occasions I had to stop but I do remember, one moonlit night, calling as booked with the London Mail, bunker first on an N1. We came to rest opposite the chimney of a superheated N1 which had stuck in the same place. I could see the fireman having a good poke at the fire, hear the thrum and roar of the GN blower up the chimney a few feet away, a cloud of smoke, a little steam at the safety valves, the smokebox door warped and red and then a pop on the whistle, a 'schnap' from the 'pepperpot' snifting valves behind the chimney – and they were on their way. We had a grandstand view and we could afford to laugh and say a bit smugly: "Old so-and-so's stopped for a blow up". But we knew that it could just as easily be us next time. And remember, the firemen at that time were 1919 men with 24 years' service and not yet passed for driving, so there was little they did not know about their art.

Bradford-Halifax

The story has now brought us to Bradford. From here we will take the Halifax road, a mere ten miles long and yet, in that short distance, I learned lessons that I have never forgotten. Quite simply, one climbed at 1 in 50 most of the way from Bradford Exchange to Queensbury, that extraordinary triangular station up on the moor, and then had an easy downhill stretch of 1 in 100 towards Halifax through the Queensbury Tunnel for 1½ miles. Coming up from Halifax in the reverse direction, the 1 in 100 in the tunnel with fire flying solid seemed as if one was actually going downhill, such was the acceleration with the controls left unchanged after three miles up, mostly at 1 in 45/50. It so happened that the Bradford No.1 link had a Saturday afternoon turn which involved three trips to Halifax and back – it was rostered to a small engine, a GN C12 or a GC N5. But the last round was with a double train of two sets of three LNER steel coaches or two sets of four GN articulated coaches. With such small engines this was a hell of a load over such a road, and it must be realised that the timetable demanded a speed of more than 25mph up these grades between stations. It was on this job that I first worked with Ted Hailstone. Ted was

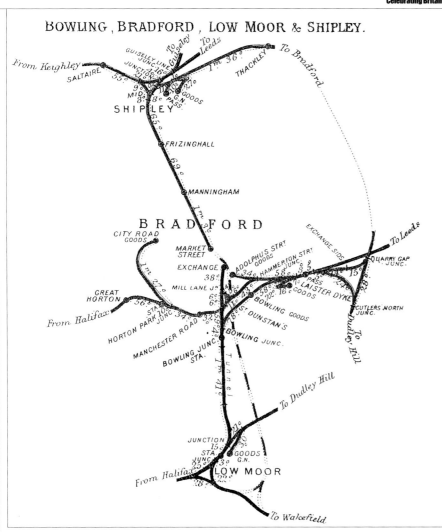

a remarkable man who told me if I went regularly with him, he would make a fireman out of me and then a driver. He set about this task with unrelenting energy and I try to apply those hard-earned lessons to this day. If he took to somebody, he would move heaven and earth to teach them all he knew and a great deal more about self-discipline. And when he had George Howard as his mate, nearly fifty years of age, they could take on the world. Ted was a big man – a commanding figure – and a very good friend to me. He was a martinet; he had been brought up in a hard school at Gorton, particularly in his final years as a fireman in the top link to another martinet, George Bourne, of whom he often spoke with great affection. On domestic grounds he had obtained a transfer to Bradford and, very occasionally, he would confess to feeling in a backwater there. Happily his closing years on the railway were spent at King's Cross where, with the A4 SILVER LINK as his regular engine, he was in his element. But, backwater or no, he never departed one iota from his dictum: "There's only one way of doing a job and that's the right way".

My first journey with Ted Hailstone was on the 16.39 from Bradford. He had undertaken to be my mentor and, having told his fireman, Maurice Saunders, to go in the train, he instructed me with some care as to my duties. Our engine was an N5 (No.5527) which demanded a thin fire at the front and plenty at the back of the firebox under the firehole door. Ted expected each round to be of six shovels-

In June 1944, a restricted service for a few weeks for some national emergency resulted in a surplus of engines at Leeds Central being accommodated in the small yard on the up side. On the left, the bunker is that of C14 6131, then we have Bradford superheated N1 4598, and at the rear is wet-steam 4581, one of Ardsley's two N1s. The men are (from the left): Percy Dimbleby and Harry Butler of Bradford off 4598, Walt Lamin of Ardsley (centre) and Harry Simpson and Harry Haigh of Ardsley off 6131. All five men wear their overalls in the classic GN, GC, NE and, I believe, NB style, buttoned at the top only to give maximum freedom of movement. PHOTOGRAPH: RICHARD HARDY; THE TRANSPORT TREASURY

C14 6124, the engine of the munition workers train from Wakefield to Ranskill, takes a drop of water at Doncaster before departure at 13.50. I was by then in the Drawing Office and hopped on to the station on my way back from lunch to see Ben Faux and Percy Thorpe. This is a classic photograph of them – Ben has the water column handle and Percy is laughing on the gangway. Ben has a cloth cap that has seen better days, a good pair of clogs (the perfect working footwear) and his overall jacket over his reefer. Percy will be the driver for the day. What a splendid pair they were. At Ranskill other trains arrived from Retford, Langwith and so on, sometimes with an old GN 'W', a Met 'H', a GC A5 or even a Director, but there was always a C14 on the Wakefield. PHOTOGRAPH: RICHARD HARDY; THE TRANSPORT TREASURY

full, four at the back and two at the front. With very small coal and the trap door partially shut, each firing had to produce smoke which cleared quickly and it was then exactly the right moment to start on the next round. I partially levelled the fire as we left Bradford; the little engine responded at once despite the 1 in 50 gradient and I maintained full steam pressure throughout the climb. Ted's driving was entirely predictable and he used full regulator and as short a cut-off as possible.

The N5s were very strong engines and they had large cylinders, so that with a small boiler the use of a long cut-off would have dragged the water level down. On the return journey 5527 climbed manfully up the 1 in 45 to Queensbury Tunnel and,

once inside on the 1 in 100, we began to accelerate, with the fire flying up the chimney, bouncing off the roof and hitting the cab windows. With a mile to go and plenty of water in the boiler, I eased my firing and could not only watch an awesome firework display, but also cast an eye on my driver concentrating on his job, a happy expression on his distinguished face, illuminated by the dazzling fire as he stood with his hand on the regulator.

However well 5527 went, Ted was not sure whether she would keep time with the 'double' train on the last round, and on the second trip he said he would show me how to fix a 'jimmy' across the blastpipe to sharpen the blast still more. When we reached Halifax we poked about

in the dark until Ted found a piece of bar, flattened it with a coal hammer and, after I had opened the smokebox door, he told me to force it under the blower ring across the blastpipe – this was a hot finger-burning job, but what a difference after we had 'cut her throat' with that little old bit of bar. Now some of you may feel such drastic treatment was unnecessary, but we had to work a heavy train to time in the blackout over fearful gradients with a small overloaded engine, and Ted would not tolerate the loss of a single minute even on a Saturday night in the war. So, on the last round the fire was more dazzling than ever. The blast pulled at the shovel as one twisted it to ensure that the coal went into the back corners and was not drawn by the blast up to the front of that little firebox. This time we could use both injectors and still maintain steam and water, while the firework display as we climbed up to Queensbury was beyond belief. But I was soon hardened to this sort of thing wherever there was work to be done in the West Riding.

This was but one of many exciting journeys I made over that railway. I can remember little of the stations or the scenery, but one carries certain 'photographs' in one's mind. My mental 'photographs' include our departure from Halifax and then from North Bridge, the climb across the town with its hills, factories and smoke and the all-absorbing interest and character of the industrial West Riding of Yorkshire. Or one's arrival at the triangular station of Queensbury to find two other trains standing at the platforms.

Then there was the time when Ted and I neglected our duty in the blackout after leaving Queensbury for Halifax so that I ran past the advance starting signal at danger close to the mouth of the tunnel but, by some miracle, I caught the red light as we were passing underneath. Ted was firing to me on this trip and had squared up, shut the bunker door and came across for a word. We had been checked by the signalman at Queensbury and had been advised that a light engine had gone across our path from Keighley to Holmfield, the other side of the tunnel. We got the tip to go as soon as the guard was ready and, when the starter was pulled off, away we went bunker-first. But because we were talking, we forgot that advance starter until it was nearly too late. Never shall I forget how I stood alone on the quiet footplate of 5901, desperate and shaken by what might be the consequences for my driver, while Ted walked back to the tunnel entrance to talk to the guard and the Queensbury signalman on the phone. Nor shall I forget how ranks were closed on that dark Saturday night, how time lost was regained, how gratitude was expressed and that I learned a lesson that I have never forgotten – never, ever to talk, never to take your mind off the job, even for a second, when there are signals to be observed and interpreted, stations to stop at, speed restrictions both permanent and temporary to be obeyed. I also learned never to forget that the driver is totally

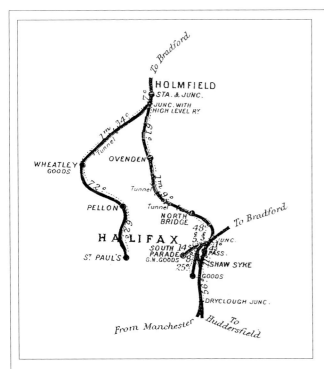

and thirsty and, as Ted was not on the engine at that moment, I walked a few steps to the refreshment room and bought a cup of life-restoring wartime tea, weak but hot and wet. I was away for only two minutes, but when I approached the engine to jump back up on to the footplate the way was blocked by the formidable figure of my driver. Ted glared at me. "Where have you been?". When I told him, he prodded me painfully in the chest and said in his Manchester way: "Now lewk here young man, when you are my fireman I'm responsible for you and don't you ever get off my engine in future without my permission." And that was all. I got up in my corner, did my job, and when we parted at Bradford he said: "I've taught you a lesson tonight, Dick, that you'll never forget." And I did *not* forget it! It was a lesson in the self-discipline which has to be a part of a railwayman's life, not only on the footplate, but in every job involved with the actual running of the railway.

Bradford-Keighley

Ted and I never went to Keighley together. When I went there it was with men in No.2 Link – George Hutchinson and Stan Pilsworth – usually on the old C12 4524 which had a short chimney and a tall dome. George was a quiet, smiling, slight man with sloping shoulders and a moustache; he smoked a pipe which he balanced on his bottom lip and would never be photographed. In contrast, Stan made up for it with his good looks and his smile. They were a perfectly matched pair and it must have been a pleasure for both to come to work and be paid for the privilege. But I also went to Keighley and back with them on 3080, one of Bradford's J2s. There were only ten of these engines – they had been built for fast freight work but, with their 5ft 8in six-coupled wheels, they were used on passenger trains. They did go round corners in a series of straight lines, but they were excellent engines. The firing had to be very light to maintain steam consistently – no more than six inches of fire over the grate and dancing on the bars. Real 'pepper-and-salt' firing.

Today I can remember little of that road, but I do remember the climb out of Keighley up to Ingrow and beyond which must have been about 1 in 45. Although that climb was severe it was a fairly routine obstacle to 4524 or 3080 with relatively light trains, but it nearly brought an old K2 'Ragtimer' to its knees.

responsible for the safety of those behind in the train as well as for the management of his engine.

That was a lesson learned the hard way. In the winter of 1944, towards the end of a very long day for me, Ted and I were on an N1 at Halifax. We were due to leave in ten minutes and all was ready. I was tired

Earlsheaton station was repainted not all that long before it was closed in 1953. This reminds me of a remark made by a certain Richard Beeching at a Railway Officers Conference in York ten years later. Up jumped one delegate who asked the Good Doctor if he was aware that '...we shall be closing some stations which have recently been repainted'. Dr.B's reply came with the merest flicker of amusement in the eyes: 'I'm only worried about the stations which are painted after they are closed'. Whatever one might think of him, Beeching had a remarkable, almost deadpan, sense of humour. When I knew Earlsheaton station during the war it was dark, grimy and easy to run by on the down road unless you kept the train well under control. Looking up the gradient beyond the goods yard one can see the up Earlsheaton starter and, just round the corner, is the Runtlings Junction distant followed by a home signal not far beyond. The down somersault is off and the whole scene gives the impression of a pleasant Sunday with the box switched out, the station closed, and few trains to disturb the peace. PHOTOGRAPH: PETER WARD

Bradford N5 5901 stands against the Exchange station backdrop attached to the 16.39 Bradford-Halifax in March 1945. I have just set the injector to work to fill the boiler and to stop steam being wasted at the safety valves, and there is just time to take a photograph for George Howard (on the left) has been passed for driving at last at the age of 50 and his young mate Hughie Cansfield, well on in his twenties, has recently been made up to a fireman. But times were changing, and promotion was soon to speed up at most sheds. Hughie was a very smart young man of whom Ted Hailstone approved. Our driver is Harold Binder, a dear friend from the GC at Immingham, and on the right is his fireman, Harry Smith, who will soon be passed for driving, a mere snip of a lad at 48. When I got on the engine on which the injector was still singing away, the boiler was far too full with steam back to about 140psi – this was a bad show from which it was now my duty to recover. Harold was much amused, and at this point we got the right away. When he opened the regulator wide on the 1 in 45, the boiler began to prime, water and steam filled the chimney and poured from the cylinder taps, and the fire was torn from under the firehole door as we struggled up to St.Dunstan's arriving with "neither steeam ner watter". Facing several miles of 1 in 50, we did not hang about. 5901 was a grand engine and, after a great deal of hard work, and much to Harold's amusement, when we reached the top at Queensbury we were on time! PHOTOGRAPH: RICHARD HARDY; THE TRANSPORT TREASURY

This is how it happened... During the last eleven months of my apprenticeship I was at Doncaster Carr Loco and often went out as an 'extra hand' with the 45-ton Cowans Sheldon breakdown crane. It involved working days and nights – hard work, but I was happy because the Doncaster gang were the best of men. They were all fitter's mates; although some were ex-miners, most did not have a trade. Nevertheless, they were very experienced in the rigours and dangers of breakdown work, and there was great camaraderie. They were also united in taking the mickey out of their apprentice!

On the breakdown gang we got plenty of variety: rerailing wagons on colliery branches, sorting out piles of wagons which had derailed when shunting across the road with points changed too soon, derailed engines, carriages, a few main line jobs, the lot. There were also lifting jobs and, for example, we changed the turntable at Lincoln and, under cover of darkness early one Sunday morning, we loaded a midget submarine on to a wagon at Gainsborough. And then, one beautiful summer dawn, we set off for Keighley. Ernie Newby, the crane driver, told me to come up and ride with him on the crane, and there was no better vantage point to see the countryside on such a day. I collected tea and breakfast for us both from the riding van, did my stuff with ballast to help our old 'Raggy' get up the bank to Balby Bridge and across on to the down goods road, and then jumped up on to the moving crane. This was all so easy for a lad of 20!

The previous evening our breakdown foreman, Mr C.G.Palmer, had told us what to expect and said I was to bring my camera. When we got to Keighley (which was outside the normal Doncaster area and therefore new ground to the gang) we found a standard 20 ton brake van standing slap across the street sixty feet below the GN line which, at that point, ran into the passenger station round a sharp curve. The van belonged to a freight train, the engine of which was shunting the yard at either Ingrow or Cullingworth. When and how the brake van had started its unaccompanied journey downhill I cannot remember, but it must have had the brake rubbing. Had it rocketed down the bank at full speed it would have been smashed to smithereens, but there it was, four-square across the street, rather knocked about but still relatively intact. The signalman quite rightly set the road through the yard so that the van whistled through the goods shed and had its speed reduced by the end of the building and the retaining wall above the street. I took three photographs (none of this present-day nonsense of 36 on a reel!) and they were all good but, sadly, they disappeared years ago and the negatives with them.

As for the lifting job, it was easily done with the jib well out and the outriggers solidly packed. Then, always a lovely part of breakdown work, mugs of strong tea with bread and marge and bully beef before we set off home. This gave me time to join our driver, Charlie Hook (who was in the goods link at Bradford), on the K2 before he essayed the task of hauling the very heavy crane and runners as well as three old but heavily loaded eight-wheelers up the 1 in 45. Apart from a trial trip to Lincoln, I had never been on a K2 and therefore took no part in the proceedings; this was just as well because we did very badly for steam. We kept going at walking pace or less up the steepest part of the bank; this allowed Ernie Newby plenty of time to get off his crane, pick a nice bunch of wild flowers from the bankside and jump up in the van as it passed. As for me, my stock as a fireman fell a long, long way, for none of the gang would listen to my explanation that I was a non-combatant, certainly not Cyril Palmer who, until he died in 1965, never lost an opportunity to remind me that I had failed them all miserably!

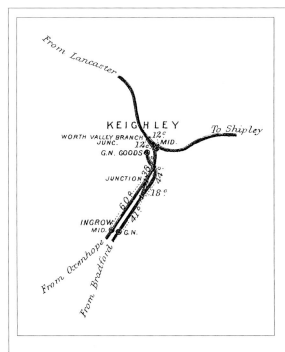

Express to Bradford

We will now go from Wakefield to Bradford on 4593, a wet steam N1, a good engine in excellent order but, in the West Riding, that was not the guarantee of a good trip. With 4593, Ted and I had not done particularly well coming from Bradford, so I took a bit out of the fire while we were taking water at Westgate and gradually built up the back with the small coal in readiness to work a slow back to Bradford via Batley. We had plenty of time before our next working, but something had gone wrong elsewhere and, at very short notice, we were told to work a Bradford express instead. Up in the Prison Sidings opposite the jail, we got the boiler full and the fire blazing, and by the time we dropped down on to the Bradford portion we were in quite good form. I darted the fire once more as we left, essential with small coal to get immediate heat, and then fired very, very lightly but frequently, four small shovels-full, one in each corner of the firebox – 'pepper-and-salt' firing, as it was known. Ted set his right-hand injector very fine indeed and notched up as high as he dared to maintain the very tight schedule of 13 minutes for the 8½ miles to Morley, for he had no intention of losing even half a minute. We started with five miles of 1 in 100/132 to Ardsley and everything was going well by the time we had passed Wrenthorpe yards and we were accelerating nobly in the deep cutting before Lofthouse station where we literally burst through the bridge hole in a shower of sparks and fire.

Ted insisted on a spotless footplate, so when I was not firing I could be watching the chimney top which would tell me when more coal was needed or sweeping up or washing the dust away but, as we came through the bridge hole at Lofthouse, I had to shoot up like a jack-in-the-box from my work to catch the signals on that long left-hand curve. There were three consecutive groups of signals on the curve and Ted expected me to call them as soon as I saw them, so I had to have the fire replenished just before Lofthouse and then get busy once I had done my duty. Ted had a very considerable presence, and as I called: "Right away, Ted", he raised his hand in acknowledgement and without a word, but with all the dignity of a Bishop giving the Blessing. Immediately after Ardsley station the Bradford road diverged left with a 15mph slack. Normally the driver would shut off steam, but Ted lent across and said: "I'll leave her as she is through the junction". He was leaving the controls untouched and would reduce speed with the regulator still wide open by using the brake rather than by coasting up to the junction. He wanted to maintain the thin white-hot fire in perfect order knowing that if the fierce blast were no longer there, it could lose a little of its heat and this would immediately affect the steaming. Once through the junction and on to the 1 in 78, Ted could now lengthen his cut off with a

Dewsbury was part of the author's stamping ground during the war. It was a Yorkshire cloth manufacturing town and, from the top of the hill at Crackenedge, it was possible to count over 100 factory chimneys in the great smoky basin of the town. In its heyday the town was served by four railway companies – five if you count the steam trams through the centre of the town – but by 1941-45 there were only two stations: ours and the LMS at Wellington Road on the Huddersfield-Leeds line. This photograph was taken in May 1949. The viaduct in the mid-distance on the left used to carry the GN line from Dewsbury Junction to connect with the L&Y near Thornhill, but by the time this picture was taken in the late 1940s the tracks over the viaduct had been lifted. They were, however, relaid in 1965 to provide access to Dewsbury GN Goods. Behind the viaduct is the River Calder. Moving across to the centre of the picture and using the Town Hall clock as a guide, the GN goods depot lies below and to the right. At the time this picture was taken access to the goods depot was from Dewsbury Junction on the main line to Ossett; this line can be seen just to the right of centre – having emerged from Earlsheaton Tunnel it curves to the right then to the left before heading towards Dewsbury Central station. PHOTOGRAPH: PETER WARD

In June 1944, Ted Hailstone and I had worked a Bradford express from Wakefield with saturated N1 4593. We had kept time despite the odds – we had the smallest coal and the shortest notice, yet we won through on a journey where everything went right from start to finish. It was a sweltering day and, after we ran into Bradford, I got off the engine and sat on a nearby barrow. After a bit, Ted came across and said "You can be proud of yourself today old lad". I felt ten feet tall, and I still do fifty-seven years later when I go through that journey in vivid detail! Later we dropped down from the Neck to the Loco sidings for water. This picture shows a smiling Ted, Fireman Harry Cram who had left his overall trousers at home such was the heat, and the gentle and friendly John Verr. Even on the hottest days men wore overall jackets, for a bare arm could be badly burned and this might put a man off work – without pay – for a week or two. PHOTOGRAPH: RICHARD HARDY; THE TRANSPORT TREASURY

white-hot, steam-producing fire still fed with the same method without breaking my rhythm.

We left Morley on time. Ted left his injector on, the pressure fell back to 165psi and then rose once more to 170 against the feed, and we were into speed on an easier stretch and passing Gildersome and into that short low tunnel with fire and sparks bouncing off the roof against our front windows and along the train. But that old engine held her own right up onto Adwalton Moor at Drighlington where we joined the heavily graded line from Batley. Once we were over the top I could take it easy and watch vigilantly for signals on 'my' curves on the way down to Bradford through Dudley Hill, round the bends before Laisterdyke

and, once through the station, down, down, down at 1 in 45 past Hammerton Street, with Adolphus Street goods yard, once a passenger station, below us on the right. On into the cutting, flanges screeching, a lurch to the right and over the junction to Queensbury, that sharp curve through St.Dunstans station, before running parallel to the Lanky down to the Exchange.

What a railway, and the thrill is with me to this day. We had done the job as it should be done, we had fought a winning battle against the odds and it was a day to remember. And yet this sort of thing never appeared in 'British Locomotive Practice and Performance' and more's the pity, although Cecil J.Allen *did* ride on the superheated Lanky 2-4-2 tanks on the

16.23 from Salford to Burnley Barracks back in 1923. That was the same sort of work – small engines driven to the limit. But there is better to come.

Bradford-Dewsbury-Wakefield
So now we will come out of Bradford with the 12.45 on a day when it was running through to London as a separate train with the probability of three or four coaches being added at Westgate. Ted and I – for George Howard was sitting in the train – had GC B4 No.6101 at the head of 12 cars, well beyond the platform end on the 1 in 50/45. 6101 was a piston valve 2-cylinder superheated 4-6-0, by no means a giant but, unassisted, it could take eight cars up to Laisterdyke and beyond, which took some doing. But we had twelve buckeyes assisted by the N1 which had brought us down from the sidings at Laisterdyke with the B4 in the rear. Now he dropped on to us from the shunting neck, but how on earth had he got there? We were stopped by signal outside, the N1 was detached, and one of the skilled and experienced shunters took us down into Exchange using the brake valve in the guard's van at the head of the train. I doubt if we would get away with that today!

Ted did not approve of some of the elderly men who assisted this particular train. He said they wouldn't run hard enough, but on the day in question we had Joe Murphy in charge and he had a reputation for tearing about like 'somebody nicked in t'ee-ed' as they used to say. In other words, he enjoyed putting the breeze up other mortals! However, with that formidable ex-GC driver on 6101, Joe might perhaps take care. At the shed George had built up an enormous fire at the back end of the grate, not from the best hard coal of Copley Hill but the same sort of stuff we had had with 4593. There was enough coal down the side and front to keep the brick arch hot, but we were not allowed to make smoke as we stood outside Exchange. So, with the firehole door wide open and just before starting, that huge back end had to be darted to get the air through it, madly and explosively blazing and banging with the flames coming dangerously out of the firehole door to be sucked back in by the blower at the last moment.

Given the tip to go, Ted would open the throttle wide and, for a mile, 6101 would be working flat out up the bank while I was hard at it, firing to the sides, back and front of that longish firebox and adjusting the injector as the pressure rose to the blowing off point. There was no finesse with secondary air because the firehole trap door, normally kept open and through which one fired, had to be tight shut to get every scrap of air through the grate and only opened when one used the shovel.

So we were in fine form and the N1 was doing its stuff at the rear as we forged up to St.Dunstans at about 20mph, both engines working flat out and throwing up two vast columns of black smoke with steam drifting from the safety valves held just below the blowing off point. Before St.Dunstans, if everything was going well

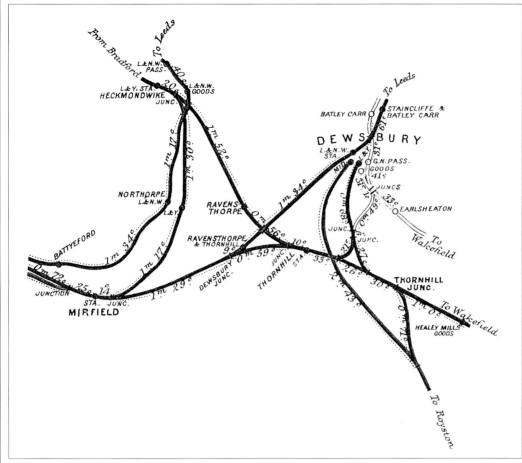

1 in 41, while the load for a B4 or a J39 was eight. Ardsley had two N1s, the superheated 4572 and the saturated 4581, inevitably with an illegal 'jimmy' across the blast pipe to sharpen the blast. If an N1 were not available, a C14, similarly fitted, would be used.

We used to talk about that old Lickey incline with its 'Big Bertha' banking trains up a gradient only slightly steeper than ours. I went up 'Batley 'Oil' many times, stopping at Upper Batley and Howden Clough, usually with four GN coaches or an LNER steel three-car set but occasionally with more. The fireman screwed the handbrake hard on at each station to stop us sliding back when the driver recreated vacuum. If the engine would not lift the train, all one had to do was to open the cylinder cocks, wait for the steam chest to empty, whereupon the train slipped backwards until the driver pulled the handle right out to arrest the backward movement. I loved that bit of railway whether I was firing or driving, and with the N1s the safety valve would lift as soon as the regulator was shut. Scenery? I have no idea, for going up one concentrated on steam and going down on braking. As for the wartime black-out, there were no lights at Howden Clough and Upper Batley – one had to stop just so by a dim old hand-lamp at the platform end. Even so, one couldn't come crawling into the station down the 1 in 41 like a half-dead fly. It simply wasn't done!

Leeds-Tingley-Batley
Returning now to Leeds, Copley Hill shed had several turns over 'The Alps' (Beeston Junction to Tingley and Batley) but they did not go up 'Batley 'Oil' nor into the 'mountain railways' to Halifax and Keighley. Leeds men coined the 'The Alps' phrase as the Beeston Junction-Tingley-Batley line was the heaviest road with which they had to cope. During the war, only a few trains ran from Leeds to Bradford via Tingley – more went via Pudsey or Stanningley – but these were heavy enough roads and you could be in a terrible tangle on a Bradford express with a C12 or an N5 if the fire was not quite right.

I remember getting on 4018 at Leeds Central with Driver Jimmy Anderson, a very tall man who had to crouch to see out of the low-set front cab window of a C12. I was given the shovel, and I had barely put my coat away before we were off and up to Armley at 1 in 50, on past Bramley and up at 1 in 100 to Stanningley where we stopped – and a good job too for we were down to 100psi when Jimmy shut off. He carried on mercilessly up another two miles of 1 in 100 before we scrambled over the top and ran down into Laisterdyke.

Ted would shorten his cut-off by half a turn to about 60%. This would take us thundering through the cuttings and out round the right-hand curve past Hammerton Street shed. The N1 was chaffering away with old Murphy banging on, so there was no respite for either Joe's fireman Len Murgatroyd or myself as, at the moment the chimneys cleared of smoke, the next charge had to be systematically spread over those white-hot fires. Up the straight to Laisterdyke we might make 22-23mph and the noise was unbelievable as we roared through the station, lurching right for Wakefield until at last at Dudley Hill the gradient eased. Good old 6101 had come up that great hill almost flat out with her boiler water kept well up and her steam pressure on 180psi all the way. But now we were shifting over the junction at Drighlington and beginning our breathtaking dive down 'Batley 'Oil' (Batley Hole); we had Joe Murphy in charge of the brake and he would test old Hailstone's nerve!

'Batley 'Oil' was 1 in 41/42, but we always said it was 1 in 37 going up and 1 in 47 going down! Anyhow, Murphy was letting those 12 cars and 6101 and his own bunker-first N1 go like the clappers downgrade and we were soon up to 70mph which seemed an awful lot more with that curve at the bottom. Even the hardened Ted, and much against the grain, put a precautionary hand on the vacuum brake handle. But in the nick of time Joe made his customary full application and, with flanges grinding, we fought our way round that curve over the LNW and ran decorously into Batley.

Off we went again, downhill at 1 in 53/89, catching Dewsbury distant off across the house tops long we reached it. We came

to an abrupt stop at the island platform at Dewsbury and then continued on past Earlsheaton and Runtlings Junction, climbing all the way at 1 in 55 until we turned the top on Ossett's doorstep. Like the line via Morley, nowadays it is all ghosts – housing estates and motorways – but we never gave closure a thought in those days when there were few cars and people travelled by train or by tram. After Ossett we tore down the 1 in 50 past Flushdyke and Roundwood Colliery, with Joe leaving his braking to the last moment for the curve over the viaduct at Alverthorpe, for the sharp Wrenthorpe curve and finally across to the up main at Balne Lane and into the platform at Westgate. We ran well down so that more coaches could be added, for twelve through to London in wartime would be of little use beyond Doncaster. Ted was of the opinion that Joe Murphy was mad, and as the N1 ran back up the centre road after unhooking he glared and shook his fist as they passed, cab to cab. This made Joe happy for he had wanted to put the breeze up the great but not always popular Hailstone.

Having come to Wakefield via Dewsbury, we ought to go back the same way with a Bradford express and this could only be done on a Sunday when the Morley line was closed. I never travelled on the evening turn with an N1 but I went with a 'Standard' (a J39); this was 2707 and we had four cars up the 1 in 41 from Batley to Drighlington. I remember little of the outward journey for the 'Standard' played with the job, but the return working on the Bradford Mail, with seven cars, was unforgettable. An N1 could take five cars unassisted out of Bradford, say 180 tons fully loaded and the same up the

Times certainly changed in the three years after the war. In my time in the West Riding we never had the luxury of a J39 on a four-coach express! The J39s were known as 'Standards' – being a large class of 289 engines they were, in effect, one of the LNER's 'standard' freight classes. The J39s were grand engines on passenger work so long as they would stay in one piece. In later years they gained a terrible reputation for motion failures and were banned in many places from passenger work. The one seen here – 64811 (one-time 2785) – is certainly getting cracking. It is passing Potovens Lane Crossing. PHOTOGRAPH: PETER WARD

Ten miles, seven of it uphill, a little engine, three coaches, one intermediate stop, and me 'on the floor' for most of the way.

At Beeston Junction, on the main line from Leeds Central to Wakefield and where the GN line from Hunslet came in, one branched left for Tingley at 15mph. The main line was climbing to Ardsley at 1 in 100 and we would slog up the 1 in 51 over 'The Alps', leaving the main line far below and then crossing it on a high viaduct which is still there today. At the top, we would join the Ardsley-Bradford main line, rising at 1 in 82 and, having stopped at Tingley, we branched off to the left before dropping like a stone down to Woodkirk (closed in 1939) and then at 1 in 50 through Soothill Tunnel to the outskirts of Batley before carrying on to Wakefield via Dewsbury.

Bless my soul – Leeds men may have called it 'The Alps' and it felt as if it was far steeper than a mere 1 in 50. But it was tempting fate to come down the other way over the flyover to Beeston Junction a bit too hard, and one evening in May 1942, the old J1, 3006, running tender-first with four GN coaches, came down to the 15mph junction a shade too fast, tippled over and went down the embankment. She finished on her side and the coaches came to rest lying on the slope. Both men on 3006 went down with their engine and the Bradford driver, Ivor Lockwood, sustained head injuries and

was detained in Leeds Infirmary. George Myers, the 44-year-old fireman, was battered and bruised (he was a tough Cockney who had come to Bradford some years before from Neasden), but nobody was seriously hurt. 3006 was knocked about, especially when the Doncaster crane put her back on the rails. That was done by lunchtime on the Sunday; 3006 was examined and dragged back to Ardsley, and everything was straightened and the road ready for Monday. There was little or no delay to traffic and the main line was not affected. Bob Foster, my old friend at Copley Hill, lived at 78 Ring Road near the overbridge and saw the whole thing. Had I visited his home that day I would have seen, in slow motion, my first serious railway accident.

The Sentinel railcars
Three Sentinel steam railcars were stationed at Ardsley and I had the privilege of working on one of them before daybreak one winter morning in 1943. I believe the car was either RIVAL or WATERLOO; both had been built in 1929 and had spent some years in the West Riding. Our cars, type 'H', had an underfloor single-acting six-cylinder 100hp engine, gear drive and a vertical boiler with a pressure of 300psi (if all went well). A Hardy-Spicer cardan shaft ran from the engine to the gearbox above the driving axle and this allowed for the

movement of the bogie, whereas earlier units had 100hp double-acting engines with two cylinders and chain drive. The water tank held 350 gallons, the bunker 1½ tons of coal, and there were 59 seats in the passenger compartment. The engine had three positions of cut-off and we needed all three up to Drighlington.

The NE men must have got some amazing work out of these railcars on the Whitby road with its 1 in 39. So they were remarkable units once their little ways were understood. I often wondered how the crew of a Sentinel lorry managed, but then they could stop and get their breath back without the whole world knowing.

In the West Riding, the Sentinel cars disappeared quietly from the scene in 1944 except when one had to deputise for the GCR Pollitt F2 5776 which was transferred to Copley Hill to work a two-coach pull-and-push set (which had a greater seating capacity). The car had had a pretty full day's work doing the early service up to Drighlington with turns to Castleford as well, but when 5776 was installed the duty was extended to cover Bradford. I remember going over to the F2 in Bradford Exchange late in 1944 and sheering off pretty quick when somebody said that Mr.Fletcher, the District Locomotive Superintendent was in the cab. However, my early morning turn on the Sentinel was made with Stan Hodgson and, while the driver Fred

Holdsworth was hammering away up in front in peace and quiet, we were hard at it on that first passenger train of a moonlit winter's morning. Behind us, we could see the showers of sparks thrown high from our red-hot chimney which, with the boiler and bunker, shared one end of the engine compartment with us. Steam, maintained at 300psi, drove us hissingly and steadily up the 1 in 41 to Drighlington with stops at Upper Batley and Howden Clough, while I ceaselessly added coal to the fire. Not a heavy job, for one simply lifted, with the left hand, a lid on top of

the vertical boiler and, with a domestic shovel, slipped coal from the small bunker down the vertical chute on to the fire below. The injectors, delicate but effective little things, were operated by minute wheels and as the rail was dry we were content in our warm compartment. But one slip and that comfortable world could be instantly deranged. In no time 300psi could drop like a stone to 200 or even 150psi and the boiler water down to the bottom of the glass as the little car struggled upwards. But the Sentinel car did a very fair job.

Ardsley

And now for the Ardsley men. There was only one passenger link out of twenty turns at that large shed; the majority of the men preferred freight work which offered long hours and payment accordingly. The passenger men ran the C14s, GC Robinson 4-4-2 superheated tank engines, the two N1s, 4572 and 4581, and, on the Thorp Arch munition workers' trains, the GC B4s. Like Leeds men they did not go to Halifax and Keighley, but they had some Bradford expresses and plenty of work to Castleford and over 'The Alps' to Wakefield, not to mention three shifts taking workers to Ranskill factory. So the passenger link was voluntary for drivers and, as was right and proper, the senior one for firemen. One or two of the drivers were 1917/18 men who had started at the age of sixteen, whereas some of the firemen had started in 1919, older in age, maybe after serving in the Great War. I think four drivers had firemen older than themselves, but there were very few drivers in the link who did not do their share of firing.

George Mayhew, with a comical doll-like face, was one who went to Copley Hill for a place on the Pullmans after the war. Bill Pearson and George Lunn were both GC men from Wakefield, but most of the others were GN men who had spent years on freight lodging jobs before opting for the more predictable passenger work. George Lunn, in his late forties, was one who did very little driving and he had an excellent mate, George Kirk, who had come from Colwick some years before. George waited a long time to be made a driver and eventually applied for Maldon on the GE section where I met him once more on an old GE 'Gobbler' in 1955. I wonder what a F5 would have made of the West Riding?

On a fine Saturday evening in May 1945 our driver left us to it for the cushions, and George Kirk said he would pass me out for driving on the superheated N1, 4572. We left Leeds Central, all stations over 'The Alps' to Wakefield. We had a good trip with a double train, and when we left Earlsheaton it was 1 in 55 up to Ossett. We were storming up the bank with the road to ourselves when, obscured by a curve, we suddenly came upon Runtlings Lane Junction distant at caution. This was almost unheard of on a Saturday evening. We were going at quite a speed and I had to make a very sharp

"I've taken a liking to you, young man, and if you come with me I'll make a fireman out of you and then a driver". No wonder Ted Hailstone became my friend and mentor, for he carried out his promise with unrelenting determination. He was a hard but kindly taskmaster who used to say "there is only one way of doing a job and that's the right way". Here, Ted stands as he always did when talking or being photographed; he is wearing a collar and tie, as did most enginemen in those days. I was the new generation with an open neck in summer and in winter. I'm wearing third-hand overalls, bicycle clips and clogs that cost me 8/6 (32p) in 1941. We are at Ardsley late one summer evening in 1944. Our N1, 4602, is superheated; it was a splendid engine and the early 'pepper pot' snifting valves can be seen behind the chimney which was set forward to accommodate the header. Ted and his fireman George Howard were working the 21.32 slow to Bradford and I was off to Doncaster on the Bradford Mail which stopped at Ardsley. PHOTOGRAPH: RICHARD HARDY; THE TRANSPORT TREASURY

This picture of Queensbury was taken not long before the withdrawal of all passenger services in 1955. The station subsequently became an unstaffed goods siding. But it was a magic place, especially in the dark (if you stayed on the engine in the warm) with trains in all three platforms. The flourishing weaving town, 1,150 ft above sea level, was over a mile from the station. By 1901 the trams were running from Halifax and Bradford so Queensbury lost some of its rail traffic, but it was the bus and the motor lorry that did the real damage. The booking office and station buildings are at the Bradford end of the triangle with a lattice bridge to serve the Halifax and Keighley lines. The nameboard says 'Queensbury change for Keighley', and that could be a draughty and laborious business if one were coming off a down Halifax train. Here is a two-coach train from Bradford leaving for Halifax behind N1 69447 (one time 4567), the very engine on which I had my last disastrous trip on VJ day. PHOTOGRAPH: NORMAN K.HARROP

brake application to stop at the home signal. We all but stopped and then got the road. The signalman had nothing to say as we passed to tell us what was happening so we assumed that he had been attending to the calls of nature. We made the time up and there was nothing for George Lunn to report, for it was our job to stop the right side of a signal at danger whatever the circumstances.

Ben Faux (pronounced 'forks') had started in 1917 aged 16, whereas his mate Percy Thorpe was a 1919 man and of older years. The two made a perfect pair and taught me a great deal about what went on in men's minds 'behind the scenes' so to speak. Ben was no ordinary driver. Never did he think and dream railways off duty, nor pass a signal at danger in his sleep, but he came to work to earn a living and to enjoy himself. His mottoes were: "It'll be reight" and "We never bother". He went to some pains to appear to live up to those dicta but, in fact, he knew exactly what he was doing. He enjoyed firing his way, and so Percy Thorpe who was quiet, whimsical and totally reliable and experienced did most of the driving. Percy provided an amusing balance to the vagaries of his most unorthodox mate who, in turn, had the utmost faith in him. But if Ben got a young hand booked with him as a fireman, he would take complete control, handle the engine beautifully, and see that the youngster did the job to the to the best of his ability.

Thinking back, I recall the first time I saw Ben in action. It must have been the first time I travelled from Wakefield to Bradford. I was riding in the front brake of the Bradford portion of the 12.57 ex-Doncaster and I noticed that the fireman was wearing his overall jacket over his reefer and a cloth cap over his nose, while the driver – who was a very tall man – was well into his forties wearing a bright green cloth cap. It was an interesting partnership. The engine, 4572, gradually faded but regained steam and water at Morley. I remember, too, that 'Green Cap' had thrashed the engine up the bank. This had taken place a couple of years before I met Ben for the first time. He was for sure the 'fireman' on 4572 on that day, and his mate's name turned out to be Roper.

But that misty autumn morning at Doncaster, when I was waiting for the return of the Ranskill at 08.11, I was to meet Ben. He now had Percy Thorpe with him. When they reappeared after taking water from the column, l showed my pass to the driver (Percy) while the fireman (Ben) said: "As ta had hold before?". I said that I had, but not on this job. He answered that I had better get cracking and, after ordering: "Look after him, Percy", he got up on the tank top out of the way and left us to it. The engine was 6124, a C14. It was a good engine, but my first task was to find Bentley station at which I had never stopped as it was closed to all but

those of the Ranskill munition workers who lived thereabouts. I was told to run well up at Bentley so that the back of the train was clear of the level crossing. The rest of the journey to Wakefield went very happily with two most agreeable companions who told me to come whenever I could.

And so I did, many times, and I learned much of the ways of the railway from two such uninhibited men. However, Ted Hailstone, who was the antithesis of Ben, did not approve and said: "I don't know what you can see in that Faux". Nevertheless, Ben became my mentor in a way that Ted could never have brought himself to be. He showed me how the rules, though not necessarily the rule book, could be bent to advantage and, although I am sure he did not go out of his way to influence me, I began to learn some of the tricks of the trade. We would go to Thorp Arch on the night turn with an 'Immingham' with our load of munition workers, many of them girls from Wakefield, Normanton and Castleford. Percy and I would share the work while Ben occupied himself with some dilettante supervision from the fireman's corner. In the early hours and well before time to get the workers home, we would be back at Westgate and, having put the stock in Balne Lane sidings, Ben and Percy were free to go to Ardsley light engine, put the B4 away and go home. However, Ben might consult his watch and announce: "Percy, we'll stay here a few minutes". When he eventually arrived at Ardsley it was just too late to put the engine away without making overtime. If there were men in the cabin, a set would be given the job of doing the fire, smokebox and so on while Ben and Percy slipped off home. This trick was as old as the hills and a good foreman knows how to deal with it, but the point is that it opened my eyes to some of the manoeuvres that take place in a man's world that others would never let me see.

Thorp Arch is near Wetherby and, after leaving Castleford, we reached the factory by way of Monk Fryston, Sherburn-in-Elmet, Church Fenton, Tadcaster and Newton Kyme and we entered another world, a level road along which we used to nip at about 55-60mph and where most of the station names were alien to the industrial West Riding. At Thorp Arch we ran across the up main line into the factory and round the circular railway controlled by colour light signals, calling at the four stations which were unsheltered platforms: Walton, Roman Road, Ranges and River. Our passengers would go off to work, we would take the empties to the carriage sidings near the main line, run round a triangle controlled by Thorp Arch signalbox and on to our train once more. There was time for a bite and a cup of tea and then we were off round the circle, tender-first, to pick up the home-going workers.

At River, one summer night, I can still hear Ben talking to the passengers who were 'persuading' him to get them back home at some ridiculously early hour – we were only scheduled to set down, and as it was the early hours of a Monday morning we had the railway to ourselves. By this time Ben had a new mate, Jim Heald. Ben announced that neither Jim nor I could run a train fast enough to qualify for the collection that he hoped was going to be made. So he would show us how to do it, and this young hand had to get a large fire going as we ran round our train once more at Thorp Arch. Much of the detail of the journey home has gone from my mind, but my task was simple – I had to shovel coal to keep pace with Ben's activities and to hang on, especially at 'Taddy' and Church Fenton where we seemed to be going rather faster than usual. We were home in good time. Ben got down and his cap was filled with coppers, sweets and so on, and I caught the Sheffield Mail home to Doncaster. After only a few hours in bed it was back to work in the Doncaster Locomotive Drawing Office. Looking back, I am not surprised that I was a very ordinary draughtsman and made my career instead in the Running Department of the LNER and BR!

New Year's Eve 1944 was a Sunday night, the blackout had been eased, and I was at Bradford Exchange in the company of Ben, Percy and Alistair Kerr. Alistair was wise in the ways of the railway in general and Ben and Percy in particular. We were all in good spirits and Ben had brought cigars for us. We had a J39, 2707, just the engine for the Mail on a Sunday night which was made up to six buckeyes and a van. Ten minutes before we started, Ben said: "Nah then, Dick will do the driving and Mr.Kerr the firing. And no messing about, Dick – you've got to knock her about to keep time with this load and you'll have to run hard down 'Batley 'Oil'. It was pitch dark, and there were no signals at Upper Batley or at the sharp curve over the LNW at the bottom. Percy opined quietly to Alistair: "That lot over there are going to try to get us down but we'll see to that, won't we?". So away we went, Alistair firing for all he was worth, Ben driving me on until, on the 1 in 55 of Ossett bank, I lifted the catch of the reversing screw which wound itself into full travel at nearly 30mph. This was the only time I have done such a thing. At Wakefield we threaded our way – much to the detriment of the crossovers – in a series of straight lines. Our arrival was exciting and typical of a rough old 'Standard'. When we stopped we knew had shared an unforgettable experience. The noise, pure thrill and primaeval excitement of that journey as living parts of that bucking, lurching, coal-devouring, fire-throwing engine will always be with Alistair and me. Ben Faux was a unique railwayman who did things his way, and

N1 69474 and its two-coach train stand at the Keighley bound platform at Queensbury. The lattice bridge and booking office can be clearly seen, but the signal box is out of sight at the Bradford end, on the down side. There were, of course, starting signals controlling the triangle crossings. and in the Halifax direction there was an advanced starting signal, the position of which, at the entrance to Queensbury Tunnel, will live with me for ever. The largest employer in Queensbury was Messrs. John Foster whose Black Dyke Mills band was – nay, still is – world famous. It is only recently that I learned where the Black Dyke Mills were situated; back in the days when I was working on the railways in the area, us loco men were usually too busy getting there to indulge in local geography lessons! PHOTOGRAPH: NORMAN K.HARROP

he provided both Alistair and me with many marvellous memories.
..........oooooOOOooooo..........

This is but a short story of the GN lines in the West Riding during the war years. They were 'bylines' to those who did not know them, but vibrant schools of teaching for those who wanted to learn. I have not mentioned freight work, for my limited spare time and its inaccessibility made it almost impossible. Indeed, I had little loose-coupled freight experience until I went to King's Lynn and South Lynn and later on to Woodford in 1949 when the Annesley 'Runners' were in their prime. Stopping at the top to pin down brakes or thundering uphill at walking speed was a part of the life of the 'Tangos' (J50s) that covered most of the freight work along with the J39s, the 'A' engines (J6s) and those old fire-throwing 'B' engines (J3s), with their small fireboxes which were often used on the lesser Bradford and Ardsley passenger jobs. Above all, I look back on men who took an endlessly kindly interest in me, who were hardly, if ever, put out by my interest, and who gave me a wonderful grounding in their part of the great practical scheme of things that was the running of the railway which one recalls with such pride and happiness, not to mention a great sense of achievement.

Author's note: Several West Riding friends have helped me with the text, content and photographs. These include a very old friend, Alistair Kerr, once of Wakefield, Michael Gordon of Wrenthorpe North, Peter Ward, once of Ossett, and Peter Rose, a retired railwayman who served BR in the Leeds District.

Right. J1 3005 had been built in 1908 for fast freight and secondary passenger work. Here, she has just come off the turntable at Wakefield Westgate prior to working a Bradford express via Morley. The turntable is in what had been the GC Loco up by Balne Lane. Before the war the Bradford J1s had often taken heavily loaded excursions to the seaside – Scarborough, Bridlington, Cleethorpes and Skegness – and had thrived on those jobs. They were free steaming, fire throwing and strong, and Driver George Stoyles of Bradford No.2 link gave 3005 a pasting back in May 1943. George Barker had a hectic time with the shovel and our illuminated passage of Gildersome Tunnel was unforgettable, with lumps of red-hot coal bouncing off the low roof and hitting the boiler and cab windows. PHOTOGRAPH: RICHARD HARDY; THE TRANSPORT TREASURY

Bottom right. Here is that old Bradford faithful 69474 (one-time 4594) on which I covered many miles in happier circumstances. This picture shows Wilsden station which was near the hamlet of Harecroft but two miles away from Wilsden itself. The two-coach train is probably fitted with that lethal quick-acting vacuum brake which applied the brakes fully if you were remotely heavy-handed when running into a station. It seems that not only the driver but also the fireman was determined to be in on the act for the photographer. Nobody ever photographed us during the war; this was a pity as there was much of interest going on and the railway industry as a whole was doing miracles in moving freight traffic. PHOTOGRAPH: NORMAN K.HARROP

Below. North Bridge Halifax in BR days, and there have been a few changes since my time in the area during the war – the station nameboards for example, the length of the train and the quality of the coal on the N1's bunker. In my day we were lucky on a Bradford or Ardsley engine to have a knob of coal the size of one's fist. The only time a coal hammer was used was to draw the dust forward when it had stuck to the sides of the bunker. Here, the N1 has brought its train from Halifax Old – that is where we used to mix it with the 'Lanky' which turned off right-handed for Low Moor, Laisterdyke and Leeds while we crossed the arches above the town at 1 in 69 and 130, shutting off before we reached the North Bridge and in good form to tackle the 2½ miles of 1 in 45 up to Queensbury Tunnel. I always enjoyed the attack on this bank with the two stops Ovenden and Holmfield in the middle. PHOTOGRAPH: NORMAN K.HARROP

FOURUM
Four fine photos from Mr.Ford

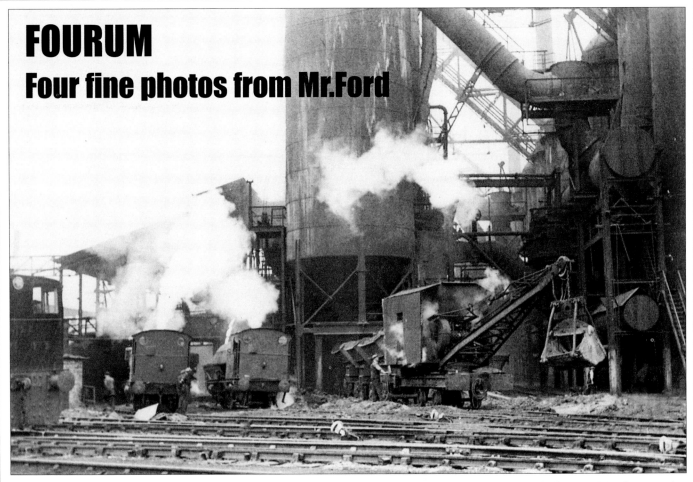

The name of W.J.FORD should be familiar to readers of *Railway Bylines* magazine as we regularly feature his photographs. One thing we rather like about his photographs is that they often show, not just locomotives, but also their working environment. That is well and truly evidenced here. This splendid picture was taken at Irlam Steel Works (part of the Lancashire Steel Corporation) on 21 August 1955. The works had an extensive railway system; indeed, Mr.Ford's notebook records no less than *twenty-four* (!) LSC locomotives on site that day.

One aspect of the railway scene which features in many of Mr.Ford's photographs is the engine shed but, as he was biased towards industrials rather than BR, he photographed sheds which most *Locoshed Directory* adherents would never even have heard of. This little gem is the 'locomotive headquarters' of the Cranford Quarries system in Northamptonshire. The wagons in the distance on the left are in the exchange sidings adjacent to the ex-Midland Railway Kettering-Thrapston line.

During his visit to Prestongrange Colliery at Prestonpans, East Lothian, on 30 March 1956, Mr.Ford photographed this classic little industrial Pug at work. The locomotive was, in fact, Andrew Barclay 0-4-0ST (W/No.224 of 1881). It finished life at Arniston Colliery in 1964.

During 1959 the Port of London Authority introduced diesel shunters at the Royal Docks and, by the end following year, only one steamer was left there. Mr.Ford managed to grab a visit to Custom House shed during the transition period. The engine on the left – Hudswell Clarke 0-6-0T No.91 – became the last but one steamer to depart from the Royal Docks.

Charlie, star of BR, TV, newspapers and magazines, at work at Newmarket. This and our other pictures are undated, but we suspect they were taken very shortly before Charlie's retirement in 1967.

ONE HORSE POWER

Photographs courtesy of the Transport Treasury (Quadruped Division); notes by Bryan L.Wilson

From the earliest days of railways the horse was part of the motive power scene and, even after locomotive haulage had become commonplace, some railway companies still occasionally used horses for certain haulage work. Looking at a couple of examples on what became the Great Eastern system, when the Eastern Counties Railway was experiencing what they referred to as 'a shortage of suitable steam power' in 1847 the company took to using a team of four horses to haul the 8.00am from Bury St.Edmunds as far as Thurston, and in 1850 the Huntingdon station horse regularly worked the morning and evening passenger trains to Huntingdon and back. Furthermore, the two GE horses at Halesworth occasionally assisted on the nearby Southwold Railway, helping the 3ft gauge trains up the gradient into the terminus.

As the years progressed the use of horses for hauling revenue-earning trains on a running line became increasingly infrequent, but horses continued to play significant roles in parcels and goods delivery and shunting. Generally, horses were allotted one of three types of tasks: parcel collection and delivery (for horses of up to 12 or 13cwt), ordinary goods deliveries (14 or 15cwt horses), and shunting (the 15cwt-plus class). Of the nation's shunting horses, the Bishops Stortford horse was a giant – he weighed 20¾cwt.

Horses were versatile. They could be used in multiple if loads or gradients demanded, they could operate in confined spaces, they could cope with wagon turntables, and they could go about their work without all the noise that was so often associated with shunting duties. One of the few things they couldn't do was reverse – if this were required the horse had to be released and then reattached at the opposite end. It was the equine equivalent of 'running round'.

On the Great Eastern system, in 1911 no less than 1,750 horses were employed; about half of those were 'shedded' – or should we say stabled – in the Inner London area, with 436 at Bethnal Green alone. By 1921 the total number had dropped to 1,317; of those, 1,035 were on collection and delivery duties and 282 were on shunting work. The horses were generally well looked after and received regular veterinary and farrier's attention. Their fodder was delivered by wagon from the provender store at Romford, those premises being part of the original Eastern Counties workshops. In the 1890s, incidentally, shoes were 4/- per horse, but that had doubled by 1935.

All the GER horses had numbers; these were carried either on a small brass plate or were branded on. They also had names and, in some cases when a horse was replaced by a small locomotive, the locomotive adopted the same name. At Brentwood, for example, the little petrol shunter No.15098 was known to the railway staff as *Peggy*, that having been the name of the horse it replaced.

Horses, like locomotives, used troughs for watering, whereas fuelling was undertaken from a canvas bag which enabled them to chomp while working. Wherever horses were used, proper stables were provided. The horses had regular holidays, and the Great Eastern even had a 'rest home' for its horses should they require a break from work. But despite the care given to the horses, the work was hard and inevitably took its toll; the average life expectancy of a shunting horse was only about six years.

The horse era continued, not only into the days of the Big Four, but right through until BR days. Indeed, as late as 1960 some goods wagons were still being built with a cut-out in the 'W' irons by which to attach chains from a horse.

In earlier years, on the old Great Eastern system there were horse establishments as far apart as Gidea Park, Huntingdon, Fakenham, Woodbridge (where they worked the tramway to Gladwell's and Sun Wharf) and Maldon East (where they worked to the canal wharf and to the Blackwater river wharf). From about 1930 horses were gradually replaced on goods and parcels deliveries by the 3-wheeled 'mechanical horses'. The Scammell vehicles became the best-known, and that firm was still constructing up-dated versions in the latter part of the 1960s. The 'mechanical horses' were actually fairly versatile and were sometimes used to rope-haul a railway wagon.

Inevitably, the introduction of 'mechanical horses', combined with other economic and social changes, resulted in the gradual replacement of shunting horses, and by the spring of 1967 there was just one shunting horse left on British Railways. This was 'Charlie', the four-legged shunter at Newmarket Old Station goods yard. Thus, horse working had continued on the Great Eastern system, its predecessors and successors, for at least 120 years.

Charlie had come to Newmarket from Diss. As befitted the 'last of a class', during his final working years at Newmarket he was always impeccably groomed with shining brasses. On the run up to his retirement Charlie became something of a celebrity and often had to carry out his

Above. Charlie poses, somewhat appropriately, alongside horse box M2462E. The prefix letter denoted the owning region and the suffix the maintaining one. Remember that this is Newmarket, so horse boxes were rather familiar sights here. Indeed, by the 1960s the Old Station dealt mainly with horse box traffic and the engines off Race Day specials.

Below. A closer look at the brass LNER plate. Originally, a similar brass plate displaying the horse's number was carried.

duties in front of press or TV cameras. After finishing at Newmarket he went to the West Country for a well-earned retirement.

Contributor's note: *Thanks to the Great Eastern Railway Society (who apparently classify these units as 'GG') for their assistance during the preparation of these notes. For details of the GERS contact the Membership Secretary: Mr.J.Tant, 9 Clare Road, Leytonstone, London E11 1JU. (We imagine that an s.a.e. would be regarded as a common courtesy.) Membership of the GERS is worth it for the quarterly journal alone – it is one of the very best railway society journals around.*

Right. Hitched up and taking the strain, Charlie has that determined 'I know what I'm doing' look. This picture gives a good view of the end of the horse box – note the screw coupling, vacuum brake and steam pipe which confirm that horse boxes were often conveyed in a passenger train formation.

Below. Underway... We can see details of Charlie's collar, girth and hindquarter straps, and the chains through the leather loops.

Above. Stopping looks as if it might have been more difficult than starting, but the handler's experience combined with judicious use of the vehicle's brake did the trick.

Left. After a job well done, Charlie gets his reward. We trust that it is a peppermint!

Work completed and heading for home. Charlie and his handler pass Newmarket Yard signal box; the box remained a feature of Newmarket for only a little longer than Charlie – it closed on 2 February 1969. The Old Station itself had opened with the Newmarket & Chesterford Railway on 4 April 1848 but closed for a couple of months in 1850 while the company was experiencing financial problems. The station was superseded by a new station to the south and finally closed to passenger traffic on 7 April 1902. It was subsequently retained for goods and horse traffic. The station buildings were granted Grade 2 listing but, as if to emphasise that listing is no guarantee of security, the premises were demolished in the 1980s.

Above. Charlie heads for home and copes perfectly well with the track. All in a day's work! This picture gives a fine view of Charlie's workplace. Note the original Eastern Counties building right of centre and the granary – which was once rail-served by means of a turntable – on the left.

Left. Home at last – Charlie on shed. The harness is coming off and he will have a good rub down before settling down. Inside the stables are well-filled bags from the provender store; there is also a Black & White Whisky box in the background, but who is it for? Horse of handler? And so to bed...

And Finally

Not quite Dai Woodham - Photographs by W.J.Ford

On the industrial scene it was commonplace for a locomotive which had been withdrawn from active service to be dumped on (or sometimes off!) a siding and to moulder there for several years before being disposed of. One of the many locomotives which seemed set for such a fate was the Waltham Iron Company's metre gauge 0-6-0T NANTES. Built in 1903 by the French firm of Corpet-Louvet – though its maker's plates sported the names of Veuve ('Widow') Corpet & L.Louvet – it had been purchased from France via the well-known dealer Thos.W.Ward in 1934. NANTES finished work on the Waltham system in 1956 and, in time-honoured industrial railway fashion, was dumped on a siding. The quarries ceased working in 1958 but, unsurprisingly, NANTES was still there. She had, in fact, been donated to the Talyllyn Railway for preservation and had been awaiting transportation to North Wales, but her 'al fresco' storage had resulted in a considerable deterioration of her condition. By 1960 – when the scrap merchants moved in on the Waltham system – NANTES was beyond resurrection and so the ironstone company donated its other Corpet 0-6-0T, CAMBRAI, which, since the closure of the quarry railway in 1958, had been stored in the old engine shed and was therefore in a less distressed condition. CAMBRAI duly went to North Wales, but the chimney off NANTES went with her. These pictures show the partly-derelict NANTES on her siding near the tippler at Waltham Quarries in 1959. It may not be 'Dai Woodham', but it is no less evocative.